Insider's Guide
to Software Development

Paul Perry

Keith Ermel

James Shields

Insider's Guide to Software Development

Library of Congress Catalog No.: 94-67600

ISBN: 1-56529-864-0

96 95 94   6 5 4 3 2 1

Interpretation of the printing code: the rightmost double-digit number is the year of the book's printing; the rightmost single-digit number, the number of the book's printing. For example, a printing code of 94-1 shows that the first printing of the book occurred in 1994.

Screen reproductions in this book were created with Collage Plus from Inner Media, Inc., Hollis, NH.

Publisher: David P. Ewing

Associate Publisher: Joseph B. Wikert

Publishing Manager: Steven M. Schafer

Product Marketing Manager: Greg Wiegand

Credits

Acquisitions Editors
Fred Slone
Angela Lee

Acquisitions Coordinator
Patricia J. Brooks

Product Director
Bryan Gambrel

Production Editor
Susan Ross Moore

Copy Editors
Noelle Gasco
Patrick Kanouse
Christine Prakel

Editorial Assistant
Michelle Williams

Technical Editor
Andrew Wozniewicz

Book Designer
Paula Carroll

Cover Designer
Dan Armstrong

Production Team
Stephen Adams
Angela Bannan
Don Brown
Cheryl Cameron
Amy Cornwell
Terri Edwards
DiMonique Ford
Bob LaRoche
Erika Millen
Clair Schweinler
Kris Simmons
Michael Thomas
Tina Trettin

Indexer
Michael Hughes

Composed in *Stone* and *MCPdigital* by Que Corporation

Dedication

To all programmers and to anybody dedicated to the craft of Software Development.

About the Authors

Paul J. Perry has been programming for more than five years. He is the author of a number of books related to programming in C and C++ for both DOS and Windows. Mr. Perry was a technical support engineer for Borland International, where he helped customers find answers to their consulting questions for a support program called the Borland Advisor line. At Borland he was also in charge of support forums on CompuServe, and was involved in writing technical support information sheets for customers. His current job, at a well-known consumer electronics company, has him set up as a specialist in Windows multimedia programming.

Keith Ermel has been designing and developing software professionally since 1986. He apprenticed at Peter Norton Computing, where he helped develop such products as the Norton Utilities, Norton Commander, and Norton Desktop for Windows. He further refined his software craftsmanship at Borland International developing Windows applications in C++. He currently works for a well-known company in Monterey, CA developing multimedia CD-ROM titles. Keith earned his Bachelor of Arts in Film and Video from California State University, Northridge.

James Shields has been involved with computers in one fashion or another since he was six. Currently he spends most of his time developing Windows applications and programming tools. He is the founder of Mabry Software—a Seattle, Washington-based company specializing in Windows programming tools and components. James can be reached on the Internet at mabry@halcyon.com or on CompuServe at 71231,2066.

Acknowledgments

Special thanks to our friends at Que: Joe, Fred, Bryan, Susan, Patty, and everybody "behind the scenes." Without these fine individuals, you wouldn't have this completed book in your hands.

Trademarks

We'd like to Hear from You!

As part of our continuing effort to produce books of the highest possible quality, Que would like to hear your comments. To stay competitive, we *really* want you, as a computer book reader and user, to let us know what you like or dislike most about this book or other Que products.

You can mail comments, ideas, or suggestions for improving future editions to the address below, or send us a fax at (317) 581-4663. For the on-line inclined, Macmillan Computer Publishing now has a forum on CompuServe (enter **GO QUEBOOKS** at any prompt) through which our staff and authors are available for questions and comments. In addition to exploring our forum, please feel free to contact me personally on CompuServe at 75230,1556 to discuss your opinions of this book.

Thanks in advance. Your comments will help us to continue publishing the best books available on computer topics in today's market.

Bryan Gambrel
Production Development Specialist
Que Corporation 201 W. 103rd Street
Indianapolis, Indiana 46290
USA

Contents at a Glance

Contents

4 Benefiting from Object-Oriented Programming   75

5 Debugging   93

6 Quality Assurance   115

7 Software Documentation   141

Introduction

Who This Book Is For

This book is for the professional programmer who wants to learn what it takes to write an application, test it, create documentation for it, and support it. The purpose of this book is to share what we have learned about software development while working at "big-name" software companies.

You will learn ideas about software development at Borland as well as how technical support is provided.

What You Will Learn

You learn important steps toward developing an application and see how the "big boys" get software development done. We lead you from the start by giving you a method of coming up with a software product, what is required to develop and design that product, what is involved in quality assurance, how to write easily understood documentation, how marketing can make or break your software product, and how to provide excellent technical support.

Chapter 1, "Coming Up with an Idea," describes how to come up with an idea for your software application. You learn about brainstorming sessions, feature lists, interface design, functional specifications, and software wish lists. By the end of the chapter you know how to create a road map to your future software product and are ready to move on to development and design.

Chapter 2, "Designing the Application," describes issues involved with designing software. You learn about setting up a schedule, working with version control, programming methodologies, and ways to keep yourself productive when the going gets tough.

Chapter 3, "Developing the Application," carries on where Chapter 2 left off and provides more information about developing your application.

Chapter 4, "Benefiting from Object-Oriented Programming," gives you insights we have learned about taking advantage of object-oriented programming from Borland, Peter Norton Computing, and Sony.

Chapter 5, "Debugging," provides information about making sure your programs are bug-free. This includes thoughts about planning the application to make sure the least number of bugs are in it from the start.

Chapter 6, "Quality Assurance," shows issues involved with testing and debugging your software. Not only are internal testing, alpha testing, and beta testing covered, you also learn how to manage a testing team and give feedback to developers.

Chapter 7, "Software Documentation," gives you ideas for creating superior technical documentation. You learn what tools might help you create your manuals easier, how to write effective tutorials, and create online help systems.

Chapter 8, "Marketing," discusses the all-important act of making your customer aware of your product through creative marketing techniques. You learn about press releases, ad campaigns, publisher relations, direct mail campaigns, software bundling, and coordinating marketing with research and development.

Chapter 9, "Technical Support," gives you solid advice about providing software support to the end user. It discusses the most important element of technical support, how to interact with customers over the phone, keeping stress levels down, and ways to minimize support requirements.

Finally, Chapter 10, "Wrapping It Up," gives you additional information about software development not covered in the previous chapters. You find out about useful bits of information that don't fit in other areas of the book.

Our Qualifications

We have been involved with the development of commercial software for several years, and we have seen how it is done from the inside. Although we might not be experts at every detail of software development, we have had valuable experience with many aspects as well as with others who are very good in their field.

Paul started at Borland International in developer support, where he developed training programs for technicians, wrote technical information sheets for developers, and provided paid-support for fortune 500 customers. He is also the author of a number of best-selling computer programming books. His books have been translated to several international markets including Spain and Czechoslovakia. He has readers around the world including Great Britain, Japan, Australia, and Russia.

Keith began at Peter Norton Computing (now Symantec) as employee number 12. He co-developed the Norton Commander and worked on the Norton Desktop for Windows. He then moved to Borland, where he worked on Sidekick for Windows as well as an internal object oriented framework.

Both of us now work at Sony Electronic Publishing, developing multimedia applications for Windows. We both worked on the *Mayo Clinic Total Heart* CD-ROM. Paul worked on the *Haldeman Diaries* CD-ROM and Keith was senior software engineer for *ABC News Interactive Earthquake*.

Why This Book Was Written

We wrote this book to help you overcome some of the obstacles we encountered while we learned about software development. It is our sincere hope that, by providing you with examples of the experiences we have been through, it will make your job easier.

Chapter 1

Coming Up with an Idea

In this first chapter of the *Insider's Guide to Software Development* we'll take a look at how software is formulated and talk about these concepts:

- Software products begin with an initial idea.

- A good initial idea comes from examining what the product is expected to do and who will be using it.

- Brainstorming is useful for creating a list of desired product features (wish list).

- The final list of features to be in the product is drawn from the wish list.

Behind every successful software title lies a great idea. Many times these initial ideas are carefully sculpted responses to market needs; other times they are back-of-the-napkin sketches spontaneously developed by a thoughtful individual. In the case of commercial software, this initial idea is usually a response to a perceived problem. The software is developed to provide a solution to something that just doesn't work the best it can.

The Initial Idea

The idea is usually based on a premise of "What if...?" or "Why can't...?" For instance, the initial idea for the Norton Desktop for Windows came from a single individual who believed that: 1) The latest version of Windows (3.0) was going to be very successful; and 2) A window of opportunity existed in which we could provide a better desktop than that shipped with Windows—Program Manager and File Manager.

This person thought that by integrating these two entities into a single, seamless tool, we could provide users with a better way of accessing and manipulating the data and programs on their computers. He asked the questions, "What if we combined Program Manager and File Manager into one?" and "Why can't we have an integrated means of dealing with our data and programs in Windows?" These two simple questions formed the basis of what was to become a hugely successful piece of software.

Of course, the same could be said about Peter Norton's original UnErase program. He realized, after examining the IBM PC's technical documentation, the data in files erased from a diskette wasn't actually lost, just sort of crinkled up and tossed aside, hidden from view. He asked the question, "What if you could recover the data from a file you've erased?" This single question formed the basis for what was to become one of the most successful PC programs ever. It provided the vehicle whereby Peter Norton Computing, Inc. pioneered, then set the standard for, the lucrative computer utility industry over the next several years.

The Tag Line

From the initial idea often comes the program's *tag line*—the brief synopsis of what the program does and why anyone would want it. It's sort of like the short description of a television program or movie listed in *TV Guide*: you usually know after reading the synopsis if the story is something that will interest you. Sometimes the story may not seem really that attractive, but a favorite star or director will lure you into viewing the film or TV show anyway.

As you'll see later on in the book, the successful marketing of software is largely dependent on how good the marketers are in describing why someone should buy the product they're selling. If the initial idea is something that can't easily be communicated, chances are marketing the final shipping product also won't be easily communicated.

A Successful Idea: Borland's Sidekick

As another example of a successful product that started from a simple idea, take Borland's flagship Sidekick program. It was one of the first to utilize the terminate-and-stay-resident (TSR) service of Microsoft's DOS. This TSR service (sometimes called *function*) was at the time a little-known part of the operating system. The designers of Sidekick had the idea of exploiting this function within the operating system to open up a new category of application software.

Note

For all those Windows users out there, remember that DOS is a single-tasking operating system, whereby only one program can be run at a time. Windows, on the other hand, allows you to run more than one program simultaneously. (It is interesting to our discussion here to note the initial idea behind Windows encompassed not only this ability to multi-task, but also to access and manipulate computer data in a graphical manner—by means of pictures—instead of through a solely descriptive manner—by means of text characters, as is the case in DOS.)

Prior to version 3.x of Windows we were pretty much stuck in a single-tasking environment, where only one program could be run at a time. (OK, there were obviously multi-tasking environments prior to Windows 3.0 on the PC, like TopView, DesqView, and OS/2 Presentation Manager. We'll use Windows here as the milestone for our discussion because it became the most successful of the multi-tasking and Graphical User Interface (GUI) environments.) But through this TSR service in DOS, a program could lie dormant until it needed to be awakened into action, a rudimentary form of multi-tasking.

This is exactly what the original Sidekick did: the first time it was run, it utilized the DOS TSR service to allow a small core of the program to hang around until the user pressed a certain key combination to bring the full program to life. Once active, the user could access the utilities that Sidekick offered: a calculator, a notepad, and other on-demand tools that certainly became handy without having to continually shut down the current program.

From the simple questions of "What if you could access a calculator while working on a word processing document?" and "Why can't we run more than one program—and therefore not be limited to one set of information—at a time?" came another hugely successful product.

Another Successful Case: Porting Existing Software

Not all ideas eventually become great successes, of course. Sometimes the idea for a product takes the form of developing a new version of an existing product for a different platform or operating system. The success or failure of the port is often dependent on whether the developers take full advantage of the "native" platform for which they're targeting their product. You have to keep in mind who is to be using your software—who your intended "audience" is. Each platform or operating system should be treated as if it were a completely different medium, each with its own set of strengths and weaknesses, its own palette of colors, and its own means of communicating to the user of your software.

A company like Claris, for example, seems to have a good handle on developing software for both platforms. You feel as if the product was specifically designed for the environment you're using it in. Yet, because the interface is consistent between both the Mac and the PC versions, when you need to, you can use the software in either environment.

The designers of FileMaker, for example, knew the target audience of their software was people working in a corporate environment, one in which both Macs and PCs were used. On any given day, workers may need to use the software on either machine. With FileMaker this is a rather easy process. However, the designers also knew that they didn't want to constrain themselves to only this corporate computing environment; they also wanted to sell their software to individual users who, for the most part, have only one computer. By tailoring their software for the platform on which it was intended to be used, and by maintaining a consistency between the two versions, the designers of FileMaker were able to develop a product that could successfully be used in either or both environments.

An Unsuccessful Idea: Software without an Identity

One important consideration here is that although your initial idea may change slightly as it is developed, be very careful it doesn't stray too far off its original intended path. A product we worked on at Borland that never saw the light of day suffered from what seemed like a wandering identity. Over the course of a year-and-a-half of development this product's focus shifted rather drastically.

This may have been partly because the product was rather ill-defined from the beginning. It was initially designed as a collection of applications bound in a notebook metaphor with personnel in the corporate environment as our target audience.

However, after we had already begun development of the product, Lotus Development came out with its "Organizer" that was aimed at the same audience. Because of this we had to go back to the drawing board and rethink a few things, add some things, and take other things out. We redesigned our application as a personal information manager (PIM).

Shortly after we had redesigned the product in light of Lotus' Organizer, senior management at Borland decided we would not try to target our product in the same category as Lotus' product. We would try to market our product as an integrated application, competing against Microsoft Works.

Because we'd started off with a completely different design, we didn't have all the applications available that we would need to compete against Works. We needed to again redesign our application, this time to compete not just in another product category, but for a different audience as well. The product was now going to be a collection of applications targeted for the inexperienced home computer user.

Unfortunately, it became apparent that the architecture of this product wasn't appropriate for the new target audience. The program was large and cumbersome to use. In order to be successful as a mass-appeal product, it would be necessary to completely redesign and re-architect the program to make it small and easy to use.

We couldn't figure out whether this product was to be a collection of applications in a notebook metaphor, a personal information manager, an integrated set of applications, or a bunch of nifty programs the mass-market home computer user might find handy.

Coming Up with a Good Idea

To avoid a meandering definition for your product, it's important to remember that software is intended to do *something* and is to be used by *someone*.

When coming up with an idea for a program, focus on two things:

- The kind of problem your software solves

- Who will use your software

For example, a productivity tool like a word processor provides a solution to enhancing productivity in the workplace; a game, on the other hand, solves the problem of engaging and entertaining its users.

A productivity tool might be designed to be used by a middle-aged manager in a corporate environment, whereas a game might be designed to be used by that same manager's teenager.

So, always concentrate on what your program will do and who will be using it. If your software solves a particular problem for a particular group of people, you just might have a successful program on your hands.

From an initial seed idea grows the fruit that will later become the completed software product. Along the way the plant needs nourishment and tending. The idea is just the beginning in the process of developing software, for it cannot exist alone. It may be rather easy to have a great idea; it is another to implement it, to bring it to fruition. Keep in mind the development of software, just like the development of a movie, is an evolutionary process; there are several steps on the ladder of completion. Each step leads to the next.

Brainstorming Sessions—Creating a Wish List

Once you have an initial idea of what your product is and who its intended users are, it's time to think about what should actually be in the program. One of the best ways to do this is to have a no-holds barred brainstorming session, where you lay out all the possibilities of what your program could be. Whether you are working on a team of programmers or are developing software on your own, a brainstorming session can help you further define your software. We'll present an overview here of how to brainstorm, first with a team, and then how a lone-wolf developer can utilize the same techniques in a slightly different way.

An Approach to Brainstorming

The most important thing to do when brainstorming is to accept one premise: that no idea is too far-fetched, no idea is bad, or stupid, or worthless. In fact, just the opposite is the case. The goal is to lay all the cards on the table, and if you've got some hidden in your shirt sleeves, no one else is going to know about them.

This is a difficult concept for many people to embrace, especially for us developers. We interact with these computers most of the time, working in the pseudo-world of code, temporarily removed from the reality we inhabit as humans. Coding tends to be competitive because, at least for most of us, we want to do the best we possibly can. We strive to develop the cleanest, fastest, smallest apps we can, to do it better, cooler than our peers. For the most part—at least as far as we've encountered—this competition has been healthy; it's helped us push ourselves to develop finer code. All the teams we've been involved with have been incredible—with some of the finest people in the industry. Cooperation among team members has been there as well: the sharing of knowledge, code, algorithms, and techniques flowed freely, as it naturally should. The competition is there to push you forward, and has never been a hindrance, as we've fortunately encountered so far.

Competition is good when you're actually developing the code, but in the formative stages of the project it can be a stifling ingredient, one that prevents you from bringing your program to its full potential. Remember, your goal is to expose as much as you can about what should go into your program. For a team, you need to get as many minds thinking, and as many voices speaking those thoughts as you can. As a lone developer, you need to bounce your ideas off as many people as you can for the same reason.

The Brainstorming Meeting

For a team of developers, the best approach we've found is to have a no-holds barred, fun-fest, limitless meeting. If you can arrange it, we've found the best results come from a weekend retreat where the focus is limited to brainstorming about the product. This works especially well if it's out-of-town, perhaps at a vacation spot not too far from home. Once, shortly after Symantec acquired Peter Norton Computing, all the developers in the company got together in Tahoe for this very reason.

Of course, it may not always be convenient or monetarily prudent to ship everyone out of town. In this case, you should make it as close as you can to being away from work, because brainstorming is a completely different endeavor than our normal work. Maybe a conference room at a local hotel large enough to hold all the team members can be utilized. If not, at least reserve a meeting room within the company in which to have the brainstorming session. If you work in a less structured environment, on a small team or in a small company, you might find it best to have it at someone's house. The point is you're going to need someplace to assemble, however many people are on the team, and let them have a go at it.

A Meeting without Limits

Having a place in which to do the brainstorming session is just the beginning. As was said above, the ideal is to provide for an open-ended meeting. This is why the retreat works so well, because you're not trying to cram everything into one session, one that may not be enough to accomplish all you need to do. But even if you can't do a retreat, again try to get as close as you can to it: schedule your brainstorming as an all-day, or a series of all-day meetings, maybe even as after-hours pizza fests. This is exactly what we did in the early days of Peter Norton Computing. We'd order pizza and talk and think about what we were about to develop. It wasn't as formalized then as it became when we got around to brainstorming about the Norton Desktop for Windows, but it was still fun—and pretty fruitful as well.

Once you have a place and a time for this meeting, you need to prepare the team for the session. It's helpful to open the meeting up not only to the developers, but to the marketing people, the documentation folks, and especially the people with the closest ties to the users of the products, the technical support staff. If this is the first time a brainstorming session is being done in your company, you may need to take a little more effort at the beginning to establish the groundrules for the participants. The goal is to provide a safe place where people can express themselves freely, with little or no self-censorship. Although someone will lead the meeting, the leader is more of a moderator, a coach standing on the sideline and motivating his or her "players."

It's usually best if the person who'll be managing the development team takes a seat alongside the team and lets someone else run the session.

In the Norton Desktop for Windows case, the Project Manager, who was responsible for the *marketing* of the product, ran the brainstorming session. There is an explicit hierarchy that's difficult to overcome when your own boss is running a meeting, which may impede on the free-form expression the session needs. Also, it's usually best if someone who's not involved with the development is the moderator because it's rather hard not to think about how you're going to implement something, even when it crops up in a brainstorming session. And the last thing you need to think about during the brainstorming session is how something is going to be implemented. Save that until later; you want to get as many ideas as you can out in the open. Worrying about whether or not something can be implemented is a waste of session time.

> **Note**
>
> Just because an idea might seem impossible to implement, it shouldn't be discarded, at least not during the brainstorming session. Very often the marketing and technical support people will have a better understanding of what end users want and need from their products than the developers might. But the developers have a better understanding of what it takes to implement a feature.
>
> For example, one of the key components of the Norton Desktop for Windows was the notion of being able to drag-and-drop files onto the "Desktop" (Windows' background screen) and have icons created that could be used to access the dropped file. Now this was something that the marketing people were adamant about having in the product; it was also something that as developers we felt couldn't be implemented in the given time frame.
>
> As it turns out, it was a fairly difficult feature to implement, but it wasn't as "impossible" as we'd first thought. It would have been a shame had we completely discarded this core feature just because we thought we couldn't do it.

Meeting Tools

As in most meetings, it's important to have all the right tools at your disposal. The moderator should use a white-board or an equivalent. It's helpful if it's one that prints copies; otherwise, you'll need someone whose sole responsibility is to take notes of the meeting. Keep plenty of water and/or beverages available for everyone. These sessions are usually rather long, so be sure to take regular breaks, maybe once every hour and a half or so. If your session is during the day, be sure to take a lunch break. Whether you have food delivered in or if you go out is up to you.

The brainstorming session should be as informal and fun as possible. If you're moderating the meeting, you should aim to motivate the participants to be free and open with their thoughts, but you also need them to keep their focus on what they envision the product becoming. Be certain all thoughts and ideas are captured in writing, first on the white-board for all to see, then for posterity. Sometimes it's helpful to tape the session, just in case you miss something.

Participating in the Brainstorming Meeting

As a participant in the session you should try to let others' ideas inspire your own. If you feel you don't have anything to contribute, that's OK. Just try to think about how you'd like to use the software, what you'd like to see in it, what you'd like to see it do. Maybe you're not necessarily the intended audience, but at this stage that's not so important. Let's say the product you're working on is a new, executive word processor (which is a scaled-down, easy-to-use word processor typically aimed at novice computer users who don't have a lot of time to devote to learning a full-featured word processor). Maybe you're not an executive, or a manager, or administrative assistant, but you've probably had to use a word processor before (if nothing else, to put together your resume, right?). Think about what you liked and didn't like the last time you used the software, what you thought was missing from it, how it would have been easier or faster to use. These are the types of things that are helpful in this situation, especially if you're trying to come up with a piece of software in a category which already has many products.

Sometimes you feel as if you've exhausted all possibilities long before your session is scheduled to end. If this is the case—if you feel as though you're at the end of the session—then don't be afraid to end it. Don't force the meeting to go on just because you've got another hour left on your room reservation. If the opposite is true, and it's possible to continue the meeting, then do so. If it's not possible—because you're in a hotel conference room, for example—see if you can arrange someplace else to continue the meeting for those who want to. Maybe only a few individuals still have more to contribute, so perhaps you could complete the session in the lounge, a restaurant, or even in someone's hotel room.

Moderating a Brainstorming Session

Just because the physical meeting is over doesn't mean the brainstorming is complete. As the moderator, be certain to distribute detailed notes from the session to all participants. It's been our experience that it's a good idea to keep all ideas anonymous in the notes, that the ideas are from all the participants of the meeting. Although it could be argued it might be nice to acknowledge who contributed each idea, it could also be a means of tagging those whose ideas were not so good. It's best to make the ideas the result of the work of the entire team as opposed to the individuals on the team.

Sometimes it's also helpful to distribute the ideas to a select few outside of the team as well, for additional feedback. Be careful, though, because sometimes these early-stage ideas can be dangerous in the wrong hands. Sometimes, some people in upper management can get the wrong impression about a product based on brainstorming notes. Release the notes to those you'd value getting feedback from. As the moderator it's your responsibility to keep track of these ideas, to ensure they are complete and useful for determining what features end up in the product. Be sure to keep the door open for more ideas because sometimes the best ideas come after careful contemplation.

As a participant in the meeting you should take time to review the notes, making sure any ideas you contributed are included and are expressed as you intended them to be. Sometimes after the meeting you may have other thoughts and ideas come to you. Be sure to pass these on to the moderator. Remember that sometimes even what may seem like the most trivial or minute detail to you may be just the icing on the cake to someone else.

Virtual Brainstorming

An adjunct to the brainstorming meeting is to extend it through anonymous electronic mail over a limited time, say a week or so. This enables people to participate at their leisure, with as much involvement as they're comfortable with. Some people who might feel shy about speaking up at a meeting have no problem expressing themselves electronically. Although electronic mail could be used in place of a meeting, it's been our experience that the meeting is a motivating event, a sort of ritual to kick off the start of the project. By getting the entire team together you establish a link between the members of the team.

The Lone Wolf's Approach to Brainstorming

If you're a developer working on a project by yourself, there's still lots to be gained from brainstorming. There are a few ways you can approach this. One way is to first do free-form, stream-of-consciousness writing about your project. Just write down everything you're thinking of at the time; don't worry about grammar, spelling, structure, sentences or anything else that's a part of formal writing. Focus on just letting your ideas flow onto the page or screen; let these thoughts be the catalyst for other ideas. You are both the moderator and the participant for your brainstorming session. Don't allow yourself to censor your ideas. Remember all ideas are equal, and all of them are important.

Once you're done with this, go back and try to pull out all the ideas and put them into a list. Sometimes as you're doing this you'll think of others, so be sure to grab them as well. Now take this list and bounce it off some of your friends, people whom you trust and feel safe getting feedback from. Ideally, you want them to contribute more to the list, not to give constructive criticism about what's currently on your list. This can be difficult to accomplish sometimes, so try to ignore the negative feedback at this stage.

For both team and individual projects, it's important to compile all the feedback you receive and use this for the next stage in the development process, whittling down the list of all possible features to a list of the features you'll aim to have in the product.

Filtering Out a Feature List

The process of taking a wish list of features people would like to see in the product and filtering it to a list of the features that will likely end up in the product can be a difficult one. Again, a meeting, somewhat more formal than a brainstorming session, can be used to allow the team members to have their input on what stays and what goes.

The Final Wish List

One way to prepare for this meeting is to distribute the final wish list to everyone who's going to participate in the Feature List meeting, and have them do their own process of elimination and prioritization of the list's items. Have them remove those items they deem not important to the product or which obviously would be too difficult to implement in a reasonable time. They also need to prioritize the remaining items so when it comes time for the meeting, a consensus of everyone's prioritizations can be obtained. It helps to keep the priority numbering range rather limited, say from one (highest) to four (lowest). It's easier to make a decision when your choices are somewhat limited. (An even number of choices is preferred because people tend to stay in the middle more often with an odd number of choices.)

The votes can be calculated in advance and then presented at the meeting and opened up for discussion. It can also be done as the beginning stage of the meeting if you feel this is helpful, but we've found it more productive to tally up the votes before the meeting and make the presentation right from the start.

By prioritizing the items on the list, you are making it easier to bubble up those items that are important and filter out those which are not. We've found that having people do their voting before the meeting streamlines the process of the meeting because it reduces much of the bantering that can occur when trying to accomplish the prioritization during the meeting itself. Sometimes people feel rather strongly about certain features and it's easier for them to influence the voting in a meeting. It's best to allow people to come to decisions on their own, without too much external pressure.

It is important to keep the voting anonymous because people may tend to vote for or against ideas just because they were presented by certain individuals. For example, at Symantec/Peter Norton we used electronic mail to vote for the features we wanted in the Norton Desktop for Windows. The results were tallied and then presented at a later meeting. Had the vote occurred during the meeting it might have been rather long, and the vote probably would have been skewed a bit.

Making It Objective

Also, because this is a quantization process, you're making it objective rather than subjective. This is precisely what's needed at this stage because logic needs a louder voice than emotion if you're to filter out the feature list in a timely manner. In most cases, it's hard to argue with the numbers. If nine out of ten people say a feature has a low priority, it's difficult to make the case that it should be in the product, at least in this version of the product.

The Feature List Meeting

That's not to say that a given feature can't be done, however. That's why it's important to have a meeting to discuss the results of the prioritization, to come to a consensus about the feature list. This is an important step in the development of the product. Again, it's important to involve the entire product team: the programmers, marketers, writers, and technical support personnel at this stage in the process. Having many minds thinking about this at this stage is helpful.

The meeting's goal is to come to a decision about the features most important to the product, to determine which can be saved for a later version, and which to eliminate altogether. Again, there should be a moderator, preferably the same person who ran the brainstorming session. The moderator may need to limit discussion of a given topic from two to five minutes so the meeting isn't unreasonably long. Detailed notes should of course be taken.

There may be some items on the wish list that are difficult to determine if they should be in the product. If you find at the end of the discussion period there still doesn't appear to be a consensus about the item, table it and come back to it at a later time—maybe through an electronic mail session, perhaps over a week or so. If at that time a consensus can't be reached, it's a pretty good indication it should wait for the next version of the product.

From this list of features of the product, a formal project proposal is often developed. Sometimes this is presented once an initial idea has been developed, as a predecessor to the brainstorming process. From our experience, though, the proposal should be as detailed an overview of the project as possible. By this stage you've identified what the software does, who it's intended to be used by, and what features will be included in the program. It makes a nice package to include all these things as a way of identifying your product.

Once a list of the program's features has been reached, it's time to go on to designing the application. By knowing exactly what's going to be in the program, it's easier to design the interface and how the program will be internally constructed. As we'll see in the next chapter, putting forth the effort of designing the program up front is going to save you lots of time and hassles during the development. This is the foundation of your application. It is a means of defining your program and helping others to understand and visualize what your program will become.

Conclusion

In this first chapter we've gone over how a software product is initially conceived. We've discussed these ideas:

- An initial idea forms the basis of a software product.

- The initial idea is usually based on a premise of "What if…" and "Why can't…" questions the designers pose.

- It's been our experience that successful software products are ones in which the designers knew from the start what the product was expected to do and who the intended users would be.

- Once the idea behind your product has been defined, you need to conceive of what features could be in the product. Brainstorming is a great way to accomplish this.

- From a list of desired features—the "wish list"—you need to whittle out the features you are actually going to implement.

Chapter 2

Designing the Application

In this chapter we'll examine the design process of developing software. Before a program can be coded, it needs to be thoughtfully designed. We'll explore these topics:

- Careful design of the software is necessary before the implementation can begin.

- A document, called the Functional Specification, is used for clearly communicating the product's design.

- Prototyping the product helps determine whether the program's interface is adequately designed.

- The internal design of the program is used as a means of identifying the details of implementation.

In a nutshell, the key to a good movie is the script, and the key to a good program is its design. As we saw in the previous chapter, software design is similar to the scripting and storyboarding that goes into the preproduction of a movie. Without a script the actors have no lines to speak; without a storyboard the director has no way to work out the general look and feel of the film. Without a design, software makers have no blueprint for the development for their programs.

Why Design Is Important

The timely completion of a software project rests upon the foundation of a good design. A good design usually comes from an evolutionary process, where a raw idea is refined and processed until you gain a fairly detailed knowledge of what the features are that will be in the program, how it is going to look, and how it will be used. Once these items are known, a plan for the development, testing, documenting, marketing, and shipping of a product can proceed.

Without a design, these endeavors must be improvised, with a resulting sense of chaos. Imagine in a movie if the actors had no idea where they should stand to film a scene, or where or how they should move as the scene progressed. By designing in advance how the actors should be situated and how they should move throughout the scene (known as blocking), the director provides a foundation upon which the actors can deliver their lines and how the technical people will record the scene on film.

By designing in advance what the program is going to be composed of (its features) and how the user is to access and utilize those features (its interface), a foundation for the development of the program is established. It is with this design that the evolution of the program, from concept to completion, rests. From coding all the way through to final shipment, the project relies on its design as a means of organizing and motivating the members of the team developing the program.

This isn't to say the design is engraved in stone once it's completed. In fact, it has been our experience that in the world of commercial software development, changes to the original design seem to happen almost all the way up to the date the product goes out the door. This unfortunate fact of life happens mainly because it is nearly impossible to anticipate all the details that go into the program at the beginning. As you see later, there are ways to avoid falling into pitfalls when changes become necessary. One of the easiest ways is to design and schedule in advance for changes you can't yet anticipate.

The design itself evolves into shape, as you saw in the previous chapter; from an initial idea grows the multitude of features the program could possibly contain. This wish list is narrowed down into a feature set that becomes the basis for the program. The user-interface design, functional spec, prototype, architectural design, and initial schedules for development, testing, and documentation are all created based on the program's feature set. The following list briefly describes these terms:

- *User-interface design*: The visual presentation of the program; what the user sees on the computer screen.

- *Functional spec*: A document listing all the interface elements that are visible to the user, with an explanation of what the program is expected to do when the user activates or interacts with these interface elements.

- *Prototype*: A quick implementation of the program's user-interface; used for determining how well the interface has been designed.

- *Architectural design*: A blueprint of all the data structures and actions these structures can have within the program.

This chapter focuses on the software's design—both external and internal. One of the most important things to remember is that the amount of effort expended in designing your app, in really thinking about it, is going to save you an equal or greater amount of time and sweat when you go to implement your program.

You'll see that by planning in advance, the software developer is able to maximize his or her coding efficiency and thus minimize the cost of the development, in terms of time, effort, and money. By its nature software development is a complex and involved process. With the right tools at your disposal you can minimize this complexity by organizing and keeping track of the multitude of details of which the program is composed.

User Interface Design

As developers of commercial software applications, we write programs for people we very rarely get the chance to talk to, to ask them how they use software, what things they'd like to see in the programs they use, and how we can make our programs better and easier for them to understand and utilize them to their fullest potential.

Direct User Feedback

In the organizations where we've worked, communication with the end user usually filters its way to the developers, and on occasion, through the technical support department. We've heard of a few companies that have their developers spend a few hours a week on the phones taking tech support calls so they can have the opportunity to talk directly to the people who use the software they write. Both of us started out in technical support, and although it's a tough, often thankless job—one that neither of us really wants to return to—there is a lot to be said for having this kind of direct feedback to the development team.

Developers in other environments, corporate MIS for example, may have a more direct communication with the users of their software. They may have the opportunity to build a custom program for a group of people with specific wants and needs, and will tailor that program to these individuals' specifications. The users may be considered partners in the development, in that as the program progresses, their feedback is essential for attaining the project's goals.

One Person, One Viewpoint

Whether or not you get direct feedback from the people who are actually going to use your software, one of the most useful things we've found to keep in mind when you design your program's interface is that you are a single user, with a single viewpoint about how things should work. And to make matters worse, you're the one who's got to implement the designs you make, and given the natural tendency towards simplicity, you may be, without knowing it, ruling out a possible design idea because it might be too difficult to implement in code.

The interface's design has gradually become an important topic and part of the overall software development process. In many respects, it could be considered the preeminent part of your program, because this is what users see, this is what they interact with, this is their porthole into the world inside your program.

The users' perceptions of your program are based almost entirely on how things are presented to them. As a software designer, your goal is to make the features in the program available to the user in an easy-to-use and understandable manner. You need to surface the features to the user while avoiding cluttering the display with too many interface elements. It's a difficult thing to attain sometimes, but with a little help you can discover how, when, and why to surface a program's features.

Interface Designers

Many companies are now utilizing people other than developers to design the interface. This began a few years ago with the rise of GUI environments. Typical for many companies, the interface designers are also the graphic artists, who were originally brought on board to do the artwork—bitmaps, buttons, icons, cursors, and so on—for the programs. With their background in art and design, they have the talent and training for refining the presentation of the program, for making the program attractive. And, since most people using computers today have grown up in a visual world—films and TV in particular—there is an innate sense of aesthetics and visual expectations they carry with them when it comes to peering at a monitor. These "visual" programming languages give non-programmers the power to implement their own ideas in "code."

When most of the applications being sold were character-based DOS programs, there was a clear distinction for users between computers and TV. With the advance of GUI environments, this distinction began to blur. And now as multimedia ascends, the convergence between computers and TV is in full force, as is the importance of the appearance— the style—of software. The substance of the program is still important, but the presentation of the content is an important part in the whole application. It's not surprising to hear many people have chosen one application over another simply by the interface's picture on the box.

Elegant Design

The basic concepts of user-interface design can be applied across a wide range of programs, from character-based utilities to multimedia titles. Given a set of features, you need to design the way in which these features are presented to the user. One of the best books on the subject of design is Donald Norman's seminal book *The Psychology of Everyday Things*. It is filled with examples of how the design of things we encounter in our life either aids or hinders us in the objects' use.

In it he explains that as users we first build a conceptual model of how to use a given object. When the conceptual model directly maps to the actual use of the object, its design is elegant and efficient. We understand how to use the object, how to utilize its features. When the conceptual model we build is incorrect, the design falters, and as humans, we tend to blame ourselves because we don't understand how to use something.

This is why software in general has gotten such a bad reputation; for the most part, the large, complex applications many of us have are difficult to use: there are so many features the programs are able to do, yet we usually require outside assistance—in the form of a user manual, tutorial book, training classes, videos, whatever—to access this multitude of features. Rarely are we able to gain full access to a program's features merely by using the software. Over the past several years we have seen these large, complex applications evolve so they now even come with their own *experts* (which accomplish a difficult task for you automatically) or *wizards* (on-board tutors to guide you through those difficult tasks). Just on the horizon we have more intelligent *agents* that will help us sift through the mass of information at our disposal and filter it into meaningful knowledge.

An Example: Design of Door Handles

Sometimes the conceptual model of an object seems rather trivial, yet ambiguity in using the object can quickly become apparent. Take a door handle, for instance, one that you might find on the glass doors at a bank's entrance. They're just simple, rather long, thin, vertical bars extending out a couple of inches from the door. Without having the luxury of first seeing someone use the doors, just by looking at the door and the handle in particular makes it difficult to know right away if you need to push or pull the handle to open the door.

You see, very quickly you mentally build a model, a plan of action, of how you're about to use the handle. Since it's rather apparent all you have to do is wrap your fist around the bar shape of the handle, this conceptual model is pretty simple. The difficulty comes in what to do next—do you push or pull? The handles are often labeled with "Push" or "Pull" to aid you in this decision process. But if not, or if you don't understand the writing—maybe you don't speak the language it's written in—you're on your own.

So maybe at first you try to push, and if that doesn't work, then you know to pull. Of the possible solutions to this dilemma, the simplest and most direct, is to have the doors open either way: it doesn't matter if you push or pull, the door opens just the same. And there's no crapshoot on the conceptual model the user is likely to build because it's a simple two-step plan of action.

Of course, there are situations where the solution can't be made that simple. Maybe the door can't open inwards for some reason, perhaps for safety's sake. So what to do? Maybe a simple (but pleasant looking!) perspective line-drawing showing that the door opens outwards—you need to pull on the handle to open the door—will work. This is sort of what has happened in the world of computers. We have gone from text— the words "push" and "pull" printed on the handle—to graphic images which represent the intended use of an object, or feature in our case. Sometimes a picture really is worth a thousand words, if it's portrayed properly.

Designing Software Is Complex

But with software, more often than not, we're dealing with large, complex systems that aren't just simple one-use objects. There may be hundreds, perhaps even thousands of things modern applications are capable of accomplishing. Designers have often gone overboard in surfacing the features through graphic representations. Those toolbars with seemingly endless little iconic buttons—like the kind found in most popular word processing and spreadsheet programs in Windows—are for the most part simply visual equivalents of macro key combinations that seemed to be the shortcut of choice in the text-based DOS versions of these programs. We had to remember those key combinations like the formulas we learned in geometry class. The difficulty in the graphic environment comes in knowing what each of those little icons represents. If there are only a few of them, and if they use readily recognizable symbols, then it is easy to understand what their purpose is, what feature they are exposing. When there are many of them, and when it's difficult to remember what their symbols represent, we're back to rote memorization when we use the software.

So, at times it can be a difficult task to surface the program's features without cluttering the display. What to do? It's been our experience that sometimes—just like you would do in coming up with an efficient algorithm—you need to first start with your idea, your solution to the problem, present it to some people you're comfortable with and whom you respect for their opinions, and get feedback on it. You begin with your idea—or better yet, ideas—to the solution. Just like in the brainstorming sessions discussed earlier, you then go over the solutions in an open forum, where more than one mind is processing the problem and coming up with solutions. It has never been our experience, however, that it's been done in this actual, rather formal manner. There hasn't seemed to be enough time allotted to flesh out the design in this manner. Instead, it's been done more informally, at after-hours discussions with a couple of other people.

Regardless of whether it's accomplished in a setting like the brainstorming session, or more like when you were in college chatting with a friend about a homework assignment, the point is you need to get feedback on your design—and the sooner the better. The more you can get the design etched in stone, the easier it's going to be down the line for you. Of course, this is another aspect of software design that more often than not is overlooked; in the real world of commercial software development you're building software for a large number of people who have a large number of different ways of how they use and what they expect from their software, and you're often under the gun, due to competitive pressures, to ship a product. There often isn't time to follow all the rules, all the time. You learn to keep things open in your design, and when you can, nail down certain things so they can't move or change later.

In recent years, there have been several design firms and usability labs that have cropped up across the country. If your organization has the resources available to utilize these facilities, we heartily recommend you investigate obtaining their services to help you design your software. These companies specialize in creating an efficient, elegant design, usually based on consultation with real-world users. Often, both novice and experienced software users are tapped for their feedback of the design ideas.

Do-It-Yourself Designing

If you don't have the resources to use a design or consultation service, you should attempt to do as much of the design as you can yourself. For example, at both Peter Norton Computing and Borland, we had opportunities to design software aimed at non-technical users. It just so happened we had a fair number of people at our organizations— in the marketing, administrative, and executive departments—who were real-world users of software, people who in any other organization might someday purchase and use the software we were designing. We went and talked to these people and got some incredibly valuable feedback, right from the start. Had we waited for this feedback until we'd actually written the code—because some of the assumptions we originally had were incorrect—we'd have lost valuable time having to re-implement the altered design.

It is very important to get feedback from others on how well your program has been designed. Design and consultation services use focus groups to accomplish this. You can do this yourself by utilizing people within your own organization as a focus group. If you're developing your product by yourself, use your friends in a similar manner.

There are times when it simply isn't possible—usually given time constraints—to get feedback from others, even if it is just within the organization. One way to approach this is to do two separate application designs. In this case, you are acting as your own critic and doing the design differently the second time. This usually results in new insights on how things should work.

The goal in design is to surface the program's features to your users without overwhelming them with too much visually. They need to be able to build a simple conceptual model that matches the intended use of the software they are using.

The best way to achieve this is to take each of the features in your program and think about how it should be presented to the user. Start with how you would anticipate it, what your conceptual model might be. Try coming up with a few possibilities, but don't stop there. Get feedback on what others think of your ideas and what they might expect from the software.

Sometimes it's useful to come up with a design, then see what solutions other people design without knowing about yours. If they design it the same way, it may be an indication you're on the right path.

To avoid having to re-implement an incorrect user-interface design, try to get as much feedback, and as early in the development process, as you can.

The Functional Specification

Once the features that are to be in the program and the manner in which those features will be presented to the user have been identified, it's time to make a document codifying these concepts. This is the *Functional Specification*, and it is similar to a movie's script. It is a means of presenting to others how the program is going to look and act.

For those intimately involved with the development of the project—the programmers and quality assurance engineers, for example—this is their road map, their blueprint. The Functional Specification provides the basis for the actual development of the program. For others on the project—the technical documentors and marketing people, for instance—this is a particularly useful means of gaining insight into the program.

What the Functional Spec Is

In a Functional Spec, each of the items the user will see on-screen is identified, and the actions of each of those items is detailed. It is an explicit overview of the user-interface design. It indicates what each of the menu bar items is and what happens when each is activated. It identifies what each of the items on the toolbar is and what happens when it is activated. If the program is composed of different screens, with different interface elements, it labels each of these screens in a unique manner, so there is no ambiguity in relation to other screens. It usually includes screen-shots—usually taken from graphic mockups of the design—so the reader of the Functional Spec can visually identify the elements described in the text.

Like a script, the Functional Spec is utilized by others in the project as a means for designing and planning their parts of the project. For example, the Quality Assurance team can use the Functional Spec to begin planning how it will go about testing the software. The Documentation team can likewise begin its task of writing the technical documentation of the software.

The Functional Spec also is useful when it comes to determining the project's scheduling. More complex items usually take more time to develop. You can utilize the Functional Spec as a means of determining in what order, and roughly how long it will take, to implement the various parts of the program.

Finally, the Functional Spec is definitely not written in stone. As mentioned earlier, typical software projects evolve over time, and perhaps some interface ideas don't pan out, or maybe someone comes up with a better solution. Just because you've already written the Functional Spec doesn't mean it shouldn't evolve as the project itself evolves. Any modifications to the design—even subtle ones—should be indicated in the Functional Spec as well.

Sometimes there are sections of a Functional Spec that change a great deal from initial design to when the product is completed. Other sections may not change at all. This was the case with the Norton Desktop for Windows, for example, because it was a product made up of several separate components. Some of the individual components' designs changed rather significantly, while others did not.

Maintaining the Functional Spec

If you're like many developers, you wear many hats over the course of the development cycle. One of the things you're likely to worry about least as you're coding is having to maintain some document because you slightly altered the behavior of a button. We've been there, and it's difficult, may we even say impossible, in most situations to expect the developers to maintain the Functional Spec as they are implementing the code. For one thing, during coding you're usually trying to get as much done as fast as you can, and as safely and efficiently as you can.

Actually, during the development of the first version of Norton Desktop for Windows, since each of us had a specific section of the overall project we were individually working on, we were responsible for keeping the Functional Spec current. Very quickly we found this to be a headache, something that could very easily get in the way of the program's development, so it was determined the best solution was to turn the Functional Spec over to the Documentation team, and let it be responsible for maintaining it. This worked out perfectly because the writers were assigned to specific parts of the program as well; it was easy for them to keep in close contact with the developers and find out what had changed. It also made sense because the Functional Spec is a written document, something writers use their talent and training to produce. There was still a responsibility on our part as developers to ensure that we notified the writers of the changes we'd made, and sometimes, admittedly, not all the changes made it into the Functional Spec, primarily due to a lack of communication. The writers often would discover quite accidentally that something had changed, and come and confirm it with us, then modify the Functional Spec afterwards.

Regardless of who maintains the Functional Spec, it is important that it match, as closely as possible, what is actually being implemented in code. Just like a script, when the actor starts changing his or her lines, seemingly subtle changes in character can have profound effects on the entire film. Through the Functional Spec, others on the project are made aware of your improvisations and the possible effects in the rest of the program.

Prototyping

Often the best way to determine if the design you've come up with is understandable and usable by others is for them to actually use the software. As we know, the actual software development is a time-consuming process; it would be costly to simply develop from a design and determine afterwards the design was flawed. This is where prototyping comes in. In effect, you are building a computer model of the Functional Spec—a functional Functional Spec, if you will.

What the Prototype Provides

Like the storyboards movie makers use, a software prototype is a means of visually experiencing the project's essence. Although the details are missing, you get a feel of the movie's flow through storyboards.

Similarly, you get a feeling of the flow through the prototype program. Through these means you gain a better appreciation of how the final project will look and feel. If the feeling isn't right, you can make changes with a lot less effort in a storyboard or prototype than you can in an already-developed film or program.

Prototyping of software is something that has become increasingly important over the past few years, probably because of the software's increasing complexity and because we're developing more software in graphical environments these days. Both of these add to the possible ways in which a software solution may be developed. And although software in graphical environments may be easier to use, it often is more difficult to program in than the old character-based environments of the past.

Given more complexity and more difficulty in developing, it seems only natural that prototyping should come into its own, and there are now tools specifically designed for making the process of prototyping easier. Some of the "visual" programming tools—like Visual Basic—can be used to quickly build a prototype version of your program. It is much easier now than it was a few years ago to design and implement a fully functional shell program, one in which all the interface elements are present, and where appropriate, like transitions to another screen, for example, actions are implemented. The underlying engine—the guts of the software—isn't there, but a user can get the general look and feel of the program through this prototype.

Any feedback a prototype's user may give easily can be propagated into the prototype itself. This is the magic of the prototyping software: It is specifically designed to allow the developer a means of easily and readily manipulating the interface elements, and then to try out the changes just made. To do this in code usually would require a bit of effort, and a fair amount of time.

Of course, these prototyping applications are complex pieces of software themselves. And, like all other complex software, they require an amount of time investment to understand how to use it to its full potential. It often is difficult for the developers to be the ones who actually utilize the prototyping software. Back in the old DOS days, many of us at Peter Norton Computing used Dan Bricklin's Demo program as a means of prototyping applications we were developing. (In fact, we liked it so much the company actually bought it from Dan!) A few of us became rather adept at using the program, but I think it's safe to say none of us had the time to become full-fledged experts of the program, ones who knew how to utilize all of its features. But we did what we could and developed some pretty amazing prototypes with the program. In fact, we had a demonstration version of one of our programs which was developed with the Demo program that we shipped out along with another program!

These days, many times other programming tools are being utilized by developers for prototyping purposes. Microsoft's excellent Visual Basic is a case in point. Given a little effort, still considerably less than would be expended if written in C, a developer can build a program prototype in a reasonably short time, and, like any good prototyping tool, modifications are relatively easy to implement. Along with this are the many custom controls and DLLs that can be plugged into the prototype with relative ease, thus expanding the capabilities and usefulness of Visual Basic as a prototyping tool.

Often, though, the prototype's developer is the interface designer, which makes perfect sense since he or she has had the time to devote to understanding the use of the prototyping tools, and as the initial designer of the interface is the one most intimately familiar with the design. Like the Functional Spec, it's often the best idea to make the prototype the responsibility of someone with the expertise to devote wholeheartedly to the task. And like the Functional Spec, the prototype is something that will likely evolve over time. In fact, anything other than trivial changes to the Functional Spec should be propagated to the prototype in order to maintain viability of the project and of the development process.

The prototype is an excellent means for other people—marketing, sales, and administrative personnel, for example—to try out the program's interface and provide feedback on how well the design does or does not work. By implementing the program with special prototyping tools, the developer is able to rapidly respond to any feedback the prototype users may report.

Architectural Design

One of the final stages in the design process is something you as the developer will likely be responsible for, because it is something involving your area of expertise, the internal design of the program you're going to be developing.

What the Architectural Design Is

The Architectural Design, like the Functional Spec, is a road map, a blueprint of the internal structure of your program. In a manner similar to the Functional Spec, the Architectural Design identifies the data structures and actions these structures can have in the program. You will be basing the implementation of your program on this. Just like the design of the user interface, the more you can attack up-front in the design, the better off you will be. In fact, you should be very careful about how you approach your Architectural Design, because decisions made here are more often than not cast in stone.

Schedules

Due to the nature of the business, there is an expectation that when a schedule is developed it will be adhered to, and it is a really, really, bad thing when this expectation isn't met. This schedule is based on the features in the program and how complex it will be to implement these features. An estimation of this complexity is gained primarily through the design of the interface and the design of the program's architecture. If assumptions made in either design are incorrect, the schedule will likely be incorrect as well. Ideally, it would be nice to know before the schedule is penned if there are any wrong assumptions being made. In the case of the interface design, this is what usability testing and prototypes are for. There are few tools and techniques available for the internal design that similarly aid the process of developing the design.

It seems that as developers we take enormous pride in the work we produce. There is a fair amount of our ego involved in the work we do. The solutions we devise are things to be proud of, for it takes insight and keen knowledge to accomplish what we do. But when we're wrong, when our solutions aren't right, when they aren't elegant, an enormous penalty is paid, a penalty in performance or robustness if our design leads to inefficient use of memory, for example. It is difficult to find the flaw in your design once the program has already been developed, because it is often not a trivial thing to fix. On the other hand, it is almost equally as difficult to have someone else point out the flaw. If this happens before you implement your code, your life will be much simpler.

In the process of movie making, the production design is the stage in the movie's development where the strategy and logistics for actually filming the movie are exposed. It is a means of knowing the who, what, when, where, and how of the production. Without this, the film would be an improvisational experience, one with hundreds of characters, involving both crew and actors, director and producers alike. And the likelihood that a typical Hollywood production could be pulled off under these chaotic experiences is pretty minuscule.

The science of movie making shows itself in this area, for if these details aren't known in advance—in what order the movie is to be shot, who's involved in each of the shoots, and so forth—the film cannot be completed in an orderly fashion. Just like a military campaign, where the director is the general, without a plan of attack or a strategy, the troops are led into battle unprepared. In the mayhem associated with warfare—and movie making for that matter—being unprepared leads to chaos which will ultimately lead to defeat, or to the unsuccessful completion of the film.

Object-Oriented Design

Similarly, as developers we need to have a strategy for taking the rather large and complex whole that software often is, and breaking it down into smaller, manageable pieces. We typically begin with the most apparent part of the program, the implementation of the interface. Although we'll be discussing object-oriented programming in more detail later in the book, we'll take a moment here to introduce you to the concepts behind object-oriented design.

As its name implies, *object-oriented design* is a methodolgy whereby you seek to identify the objects—the data structures (also known as *classes*)—your program will be composed of, and the operations (*methods*) these objects can perform. Object-oriented languages provide facilities for easily encapsulating the data structures and their operations into unified entities called classes.

Discovering the Objects in Your Program

Given the Functional Spec, we have a blueprint of the objects that need to be represented on-screen. What we can do is go through the Functional Spec and expose the objects we'll be using in our program, then the operations these objects will perform, and finally the attributes these objects will have. We'll be discovering, respectively, our classes, their methods, and data members. From this we'll have an understanding of the individual entities of which our program will be composed.

> **Note**
>
> We can think of these objects in terms of nouns: go through the Functional Spec and mark the nouns you encounter, with a yellow highlighter, for example. These are likely to be classes you'll need to create in your program's implementation. You should create a list of these classes—electronically in a text editor is often the best way of doing this—to which you'll be adding methods and data members later on.
>
> Now, go back through the Functional Spec and mark the verbs you encounter with another color. These are the methods—the actions—your classes will have associated with them. Going back to your list of classes you've identified, you can add the methods to each of the classes.
>
> Finally, scan the document once more and mark the adjectives you encounter with yet another color. These are the attributes—the likely data members within the classes—you'll use to represent the object in code. As with the methods, go back to your list of classes and add these data members to their respective classes.

To summarize:

- Find the **nouns**; these are your **objects**.
- Find the **verbs**; these are the objects' **methods**.
- Find the **adjectives**; these are the objects' **data members.**

Discovering Connections between Objects

Once you have identified the classes, their methods, and data members, you can begin to think of these as objects, as entities in their own right, which will likely have connections to and communications with other objects in the system. You need to think carefully about how these objects will communicate with one another, because if done correctly the process of developing the software will flow. If not, if your connections are inefficient, if your communications are clouded, you'll either have to rework your design or kludge your way around any problems you encounter. And a kludge should always be treated very seriously, because it is something that isn't really a part of the system; it stands out on its own. It is a pointer indicating the flaw in your design. Kludges often turn out to be sources of unanticipated bugs in your program, bugs which are often very hard to find.

As with other forms of design, we've found it is best to first think about the possible solutions yourself, then utilize other people to flesh out the design. One of the greatest tools available to the software developer is the white board. It gives a way of graphically representing often complex objects, processes, and communications in an easily understandable manner. (That and you don't end up with a bunch of chalk all over your hands!) Like the prototype, it is easy to modify when necessary.

Reworking the Design

During the development of the Norton Desktop for Windows, for example, an original architectural design to one of the program's parts, one that had already begun to be implemented in code, was found to be flawed, inefficient, and not easily expandable to support features that may be necessary in future versions of the program. By carefully sitting back and working through the design, the objects, their actions and data members, how data would flow through these objects, and how these objects would communicate to one another—all on a large white board in one of the conference rooms—we were able to quickly salvage a situation which could have been a major factor in preventing the product from shipping on time.

As with any design, your goal is to anticipate as much as possible up front so your implementation will progress quickly and at an orderly pace. If you know the details of how you're going to implement a given feature—if you've broken that feature up into its underlying, core parts—you can progress through the program's development cycle in a much more aware, much simpler manner. Having gone through many experiences of having to design on the fly, we can say that although it is rather tedious sometimes to properly design the program up front, the amount of effort that is saved during the implementation is well worth it.

Conclusion

In this chapter we've seen that through the careful design of your program, by breaking the program up into manageable pieces, you are setting the stage for the process of implementing the code, for producing the program. We've seen the design of how the program features are to be presented to the user must first be realized.

From this design a Functional Specification is created as a means of documenting the interface design, so everyone involved in the product has the same understanding of what the vision of the program is to be.

We've also seen that, often, assumptions made in the design of the interface may be incorrect, and it is best to test the design before actually writing the code. To aid in this testing process, we've seen how prototypes can be used to try the interface design out on real-world users and get their feedback.

Finally, the internal design of the program—the program's architectural design—is used to identify the details of the implementation that will be expressed in code during the development process. The ultimate goal of the entire design process, like the preproduction process in movie making, is to help you identify possible errors in your approach to the project's implementation at a stage where it is easy to make necessary changes. Once you've begun the software's development, it is far more difficult to rectify any incorrect assumptions you may have made about implementing the project.

In summary, this chapter discussed these topics:

- Software must be carefully designed before it can be coded.

- A Functional Specification provides a convenient means of communicating the product's design.

- A prototype version of the product is a useful way of determining how well the interface is designed.

- An internal design of the program identifies the implementation details of the product.

Chapter 3

Developing the Application

In this chapter we'll focus on what it takes to develop the code that becomes the finished product. We'll discuss these topics:

- The development begins with creating a schedule based on the product's features and the resources available to implement those features.

- The actual implementation of the product begins by choosing which language is best suited for developing the program.

- Algorithms serve as the basis for implementation of the product's various tasks.

- You should pay careful attention to your development environment.

- By pacing yourself you can remain productive through the difficult periods that are sometimes a part of the development process.

The process of actually developing the software you've designed is what is typically thought of when most people think of programming. It is the hands-on creation of the code that makes the program do what it is intended to do. This is often the most demanding, yet the most re-warding aspect of developing software. It is demanding in that some-times long hours are required to get the job done in a timely manner. It is rewarding because what were once amorphous concepts and ob-jects based in virtuality become real-world applications.

Setting Up a Schedule

It has been our experience that commercial software development involves a tradeoff between a given set of features and the amount of time it takes to actually implement each of the features. As was mentioned earlier, the goal of the software developer is to produce the most efficient, best-behaving software in the shortest amount of time possible.

Why Schedules Are Necessary

Software has a release date, usually known as its *ship date*, the exact day the shrink-wrapped package is shipped to an expectant cadre of software distributors. These distributors in turn ship it to the retailers, who eventually sell the software to the public. Like a movie's release, any delay in the project's actual completion has severe implications for others involved in the testing, marketing, and distribution of the prod-uct. If the development of the software takes longer than expected, it obviously isn't going to be available to the consumer when originally anticipated. It also can mean that marketing campaigns need to be delayed until the appropriate time—usually when the product is about to ship. Given enough of a delay, sometimes as little as a few weeks, the original marketing may have been a wasted effort and needs to be re-implemented with the new release date as its target.

Press announcements are often timed for maximum impact. The press serves as an important medium in the communication about the soft-ware from the software's manufacturer to the public at large. In a way, the press serves as a low-cost marketing tool. Positive mention of a software product can be just as valuable in some situations as an adver-tising campaign. Given a good enough word, it can be more effective and more efficient than a costly advertisement. In many cases, these good words from the press are included with the ads. What's been commonly called "vaporware"—a delay in the shipment of software after it's been announced to the press—has quite a negative connota-tion these days.

In the early days of working at Peter Norton Computing, schedules, like designs, were less formalized than they are now. Simply just knowing what needed to go into the programs and when we thought we could ship the product usually sufficed. Then, as the ship date loomed, so would the pressure to complete the program. There was a shoot-from-the-hip approach that served well, given the small number of people involved in the software's development. As the software we were developing became increasingly more complex and the number of people on the team increased, along with the number of people depending on a firm ship date, the need for a real schedule became apparent. Project management software quickly became an essential ingredient in the process of developing our software. It allowed us to maintain a sense of order over the numerous details that go into the development of complex, modern-day commercial software packages.

What Schedules Do

Delays in the release of the product are therefore to be avoided as much as possible. One of the best tools aiding in this is schedules. Every project has two elements to it: the tasks to be completed by a given date, and the resources available to implement the tasks. Linking the tasks to the resources provides a means of keeping track of how and when the project's tasks are to be completed. And because you can set dependencies between tasks, you may discover that a delay in one area of the project may or may not have an impact on the final completion date. Dependent tasks—those tasks that can only be started after another task has been completed—are easily identifiable and trackable in a schedule. Delays in dependent tasks will usually have an impact on the final completion date.

Choosing Project Management Software

There are numerous ways to implement a schedule. The best way is to utilize your computer to help set up and maintain a schedule. There is a multitude of software packages available for this purpose. Some are simple, designed for the novice scheduler; others are complex, feature-laden packages fit for industrial use, like high-rise skyscraper construction firms. Depending on the complexity of your project—the number of tasks and resources—you may not need the higher-end schedule packages and the detailed features they offer. Symantec's On Target is an example of this. But if you've got a big, high-budget project with numerous people on the team, you may need the horsepower of the more expensive, higher-end schedulers—like Microsoft Project. You may want to go to your local library and get a recent issue of a computer magazine that provides a comparison of scheduling packages available for your computer. This is often the best way of determining which package is right for you given your own circumstances and requirements.

If you're new to project management software, take some time to learn how to use it. Most packages come with a tutorial that provides an overview of the program's basics and gives you a running start at using the software. It may be this is all you need to know to use the software to your benefit. If not and you need to know more advanced aspects of the software, there may be books or training available to help you. You can check with the manufacturer of the software to see if it has a list of third-party support and training services. This is usually the most efficient means of finding additional resources specific to your project management software. As with any tool, you first need to know what you expect to accomplish with it, then learn what it takes to use the tool to get the job done.

Utilizing Project Management Software

Once you've chosen a project management software package and learned to use its features, you're ready to begin applying the software for your own projects. You need to keep track of the tasks to be accomplished, when the project needs to be done, and the resources available to complete the tasks. That's what the scheduler is for. Given a desired completion date, you can utilize the scheduler as a tool in determining if the completion date is realistic given the tasks to be done and the available resources.

On a per task basis, you need to estimate how long it will take to accomplish the task and assign a resource (usually a person, but it also may be another team or organization) responsible for the task's completion. If you're the project's manager, you'll be the one responsible for actually doing this; if you're one of the team members of the project, it's helpful to know what goes into the schedule's development in order to gain a better appreciation of the project as a whole.

Often, delays in the completion of software cannot be avoided. A schedule gives you the flexibility of being able to track delays, what their impact may be on the final completion date, and ways in which the tasks and resources can be manipulated to realize the completion date if it's rock-solid. This project-wide tracking of the project can smooth tensions between the product-oriented divisions and the market-oriented divisions by making everyone aware of the importance and timing of one another.

Sometimes you need to cut the number of tasks, or the complexity of the tasks; other times you need to add more resources to meet the completion date. This may mean negotiating between market-driven desires and needs and technical development realities and limitations. As was explained many, many years ago, simply throwing more people onto a project doesn't necessarily mean the project will complete earlier. There comes a point where the communication necessary to efficiently accomplish a project's tasks breaks down and becomes a hindrance in the completion of the project, a point where more energy goes into maintaining the scaffolding than goes into completing the building.

Manipulating the Schedule

There are ways resources can be added without degrading the system as a whole. When we were originally designing the Norton Desktop for Windows, we knew what features we wanted in the software and what resources we had available in-house to do the job. It was determined that we didn't have the capability of developing the software completely ourselves, that we'd need some outside help. We began by identifying those things we could develop ourselves given our resources, and then figuring out ways in which we could either acquire or contract out those features we couldn't do ourselves.

One of the key components of the software was the Macintosh-like capability of accessing data and programs directly on the desktop. Using project management software as a sketchpad, we determined that, given our current resources and what we thought it would take to complete the task, there was no way we could get it done within the window of opportunity we saw available to us. The new version of Windows (version 3.0) was in its pre-release testing stage, and was scheduled to be available to end users within 12 months. With the multitude of features essential for the package and our available resources, we saw there was no way we could complete the project in a year.

We began searching for a solution to this dilemma. We knew it was too critical and time-intensive a feature to implement ourselves, that it would pull too much away from the overall development of the project.

We realized there were two options available to us: acquire an existing product that accomplished what we wanted, or contract out to have it completed by an outside firm. We simultaneously investigated both paths and determined neither one would provide a solution for us. It would take too long, and be too draining on our resources to incorporate an existing piece of software into what we designed as an integrated package. And this aspect of the product was too critical to rely on an outside development firm. There was a huge potential for development complications with such a critical aspect: complications in communication and in control over the project appeared paramount.

During this time Symantec purchased Peter Norton Computing. It was determined the Norton Desktop for Windows (NDW) was a key piece of software that needed to ship as soon as possible. Symantec gave us the go-ahead to determine what was necessary for getting the software out in a timely fashion. We decided we would construct a kernel around which various components would be attached. Those components that didn't need to be directly attached to the kernel—like the icon editor, for instance—could be completed by an outside development firm. We went through and identified what it would take to build this kernel, which features would utilize this kernel, and then what kind of personnel would be required to implement it all. From an original core of three developers, we added a total of nine other developers over several months to the NDW team.

The success in the timely completion of Norton Desktop for Windows is directly attributable to utilization of project management software. The management team was able to easily identify and keep track of the tasks and available resources required to complete the project. It was fortunate the design of the software was highly departmentalized, so a small number of individual programmers became responsible for the various aspects of the overall package. This allowed regular and efficient communication about the progress of the project. Because of this, delays were readily identified and quickly solved so they had little impact on the final completion date. The ability to keep track of a moving target and adjust for variations to the original plan allowed us to meet our target ship date.

The Art of Estimating

Estimating the completion of a task is a fine art that seems to be acquired through experience rather than through raw talent (or luck, as is the case sometimes). You're trying to determine how long a given task will take to complete. When it comes to developing software, we've learned a few tricks in estimating how long it will take to complete a scheduled task.

First, as a developer of software, you need to keep close track of your abilities and experience. Every new task you are given is a chance to flex your programming muscles. Like an athlete, you need to know what your capabilities and limitations are, what will be required of you should you be asked to go beyond your current capabilities, exceed your current limitations.

You also need to make sure you're building a library of algorithms and routines that can be readily used by other tasks you encounter over time. If you're an object-oriented programmer, keep track of those objects you construct; they might come in handy later on. The idea here is to utilize your past experiences to cut down the amount of time it takes to implement the given features of a program.

Also, make sure you've got access to other resources for when you don't know how to implement something. Developer's journals, magazines, books, and organizations, as well as on-line services are a few of the outside resources that can be utilized when you're in over your head. Don't forget to keep those contacts you've made at developer's conferences and friends from past jobs handy because they're a readily available way of getting access to a multitude of experiences. Maybe you haven't written an AI engine for an arcade-style game in the past, but you might be able to find someone or someplace to help you get what you need to get the job done efficiently.

Here are some pointers we've compiled that you might find useful the next time you need to provide an estimate for a schedule:

- Have I done this task before?

  When you estimate how long a given task will take, think about whether you've done this task before, for you might already have an implementation lying around that can be used. It might not always be code that can be brought in directly; it may be an algorithm you have handy, or generalized knowledge that can be used to provide a solution. It may be as simple as having done something similar to the task at hand, and knowing the previous task took three days to complete, so it's likely it will take three days to complete the current task.

- Do I have code around that can be used to complete the task?

  Especially in the object-oriented world of programming, you may have created something in the past that can be applicable to the task at hand. It might need to be manipulated; it might not. But hopefully you've got something lying around that can ease your implementation pains. Even if you're utilizing procedural methodology, keep a library of data structures and functions around because they may be handy later on.

- What resources are available to aid me?

  You may not have the answer, but someone else just might. Look for help from teammates, friends at previous places of employment, contacts you've made at developer's conferences, and so on. Keep track of developer's magazines and books to search for solutions to problems. Going on-line and searching or asking for help is often the best answer.

- However long you think it's going to take, in reality it's going to take longer.

  It's been our experience that it's better to live up to realistic estimations than to try to "macho" your way through development. Think carefully about what it takes to complete a task. It might not sound too good to say it's going to take two weeks to complete something many programmers think they can do in one, but it's worse if you're consistently late in developing your software. Put in a fudge factor and estimate something is going to take a little longer than what you really think. If you're fortunate and don't run into any foul-ups, you'll be a hero for getting the job done ahead of schedule. But more often than not, you're going to run into something you hadn't thought of that's going to delay the completion of the task. Taking this into account beforehand gives the appearance that you meet your schedules.

- For the project as a whole, add an "Unknown Task" to the project.

  This is a macro expansion of the previous item, applied to the overall project. No matter how long you think it's going to take to complete the project, in reality it's going to take longer. It's been our experience that sometime in the later stages of development some previously unforeseen problem of immense difficulty, or an additional feature or requirement, will rear its ugly head and, if not anticipated in advance, will delay the final completion of the project. In the schedule, have one of the tasks labeled as "Unknown Task" and give it at minimum one tenth of the overall development time period. Given a difficult snafu, it could consume as much as a third of the original overall estimated development time.

Ultimately, evaluation of your job performance is directly tied to your ability to do what you say you can do within the time period you say you can do it. As you gain more experience, you gain a deeper understanding of your abilities and limitations and of what is required to get the job done, and how long it will take you to accomplish the tasks you've been assigned.

The Politics of Schedules—Dealing with Delays

The act of developing and maintaining a schedule can itself be an involved process, because it may mean negotiating between marketing desires and needs and development realities and limitations, especially when delays are encountered. When it comes to scheduling, it most often is the developers telling the rest of the organization how long it's going to take to complete the implementation of the project. And it's the rest of the organization questioning why it can't be done sooner.

We don't mean to paint this as an antagonistic relationship, with Machiavellian underpinnings where organizational departments are conspiring with and against other departments to further their own goals. The reality of commercial software development, as we've experienced, is that the goals of, say, both marketing and development are to get the best piece of software possible out as fast as possible. However, there may be differing viewpoints on what it takes to accomplish that common goal. And it is here that difficulties and misunderstandings may arise when the developers say it's going to take longer to finish something than the marketers are comfortable with, given their view of the marketplace.

So when it comes to revising a schedule to meet shifting needs, there are a few things that can be done to ease this process:

- Determine those areas causing the schedule to be delayed. Investigate potential solutions to complete the task within the given time, and if it can't be done, know why it can't be done. It may be that something else can be utilized to get the problem tasks done. At the very least, know how long the delays are and their impact on the final completion date.

- The details of features can be prioritized, and those with a lower priority can be eliminated, delayed, or reassigned to other, perhaps more junior personnel. Why waste valuable resources on a task that isn't all that important? From a developer's standpoint, perhaps there are unanticipated technical limitations that may be encountered and render a given feature impossible to implement. Why waste the resources attempting to implement something that can't be done?

- Perhaps there are outside resources that can be utilized to complete some tasks in parallel with the other tasks instead of serially. Ideally it's best if these are identified when the schedule is initially developed, but the resources can also be applied in the later stages of the project if it becomes necessary. The later it's done, the more profound the impact on the completion date because the amount of time available for researching and utilizing outside resources diminishes.

- See if task dependencies can be removed. By removing dependencies you are making them activities that can be done in parallel, as opposed to serially. By making as many tasks as possible parallel, you can in effect condense the schedule, making the completion date closer to the original date and account for delays.

Ultimately a schedule is utilized as a means of determining what it takes to complete the project, and when the project is going to be completed. By properly preparing for the schedule, it is possible to determine reasonable estimates for completion of the tasks in the project. By maintaining the schedule, it is possible to keep track of the various details that comprise the overall product and whether or not they are being completed in a timely fashion, and what impact, if any, delays have on the final completion date. Using the right project management software for the task at hand provides a powerful tool for accomplishing this important organizational aspect of software development.

Version Control

Because of the complexity of modern software, the number of features and therefore the number of people involved in the development of a project, it has become increasingly important to protect the development process from potential pitfalls as much as possible. One of the safety nets commercial software developers use is source code version control systems.

Version control software provides a means of organizing and protecting the various components of which the project is comprised. It is used to limit access to source code files so changes one team member makes aren't overwritten by another team member. It also is used as a means of stepping back to a previous revision of a source code file when a solution path just didn't work out as anticipated. It finally is used to bind all the project's components to a version number, so that you can, for example, easily rebuild a previous version of a program.

Like project management software, there are a variety of packages available to software developers. Determining the best one for your needs and expectations on the platform or platforms you'll be developing on is best accomplished through a little research. Often a comparison of version control software is provided for just this purpose in developer's magazines. As with any piece of software, determine what you need from it, how you anticipate it will be used, and what you'd expect to pay for it. Based on your own criteria and the magazine reviews, it's usually possible to find the right version control software for your needs.

There are a few approaches to setting up and utilizing a version control system. At Peter Norton Computing, we originally used source code control for implementing a library of common functions and data structures that could be utilized by the various programs we were developing. We needed a means of organizing the development system and ensuring the integrity of the source code modules that made up the library. We utilized a library-like system in which developers would check out individual source-code modules that could only be modified by them while checked out, then check them back in once the changes were complete. The benefit to this is that it is difficult to overwrite changes to a module because only one person has access to it at any given time when it's checked out. The obvious limitation to this is that, should someone keep something of importance checked out for a long period of time, it could have a detrimental effect on the whole project.

At Borland this seemed to be an important issue, at least for the team we were on. It was determined that it was more important to have ready access to all of the modules in the project than to ensure safety against overwriting modifications. In retrospect, this is not a wise thing to do because it's far easier to get someone to check in a needed file than it is to re-implement lost changes.

In fact, most version control systems provide a means of allowing one person to override the lockout and make changes to a file that has been checked out. Overriding the lock is not an easy thing to do compared with checking in and checking out modules, so a degree of safety is maintained. It is provided as a means of bypassing those occasions when, for example, a coworker who has already gone home has mistakenly left a file checked out; you just absolutely need this file to get the demo version out to the company president the next morning.

Should you ever encounter the debate as to whether to utilize the check in/check out system, voice your opinion rather strongly in favor of it. In the long run, you will be better protected from your own and others' mistakes.

It's been our experience that having personnel dedicated to maintaining the version control system is essential. People with experience setting up and updating a system are invaluable members of the team, because it frees up personnel—and therefore time and energy—that can be used for completing the project instead of maintaining the version control system. At Peter Norton Computing we were lucky enough to have people interested in developing and maintaining the system. These were developers who took extra time and energy in addition to their own responsibilities to design and implement the version control system we all ultimately used. Eventually when we were purchased by Symantec, dedicated personnel were brought in to take care of this for us. At Borland, support staff were likewise allocated for this purpose.

Coding

The actual development of the program—the implementation of the code—is what many of us developers feel we do best, what we are most comfortable with. Although there are many books available that address specific programming topics, there are few books written by programmers with experience at major commercial software development companies. It is our intention here to examine the practice of developing software as we've encountered it at the well-known companies for which we've had the pleasure of working.

Choosing the Best Language for the Task

When it comes to actually implementing the code, the first thing to decide is what language can best be utilized to accomplish a given task. In most cases, assembly language and C or C++ are primarily used for developing commercial applications. Assembly language is typically used for time-critical operations and for interacting directly with the operating system; C and C++ have become the *lingua franca* of development languages because of their versatility, and because there is a large pool of available talent proficient in using these languages.

For your own development, you need to determine what you expect from your program, what its demands are, and what technical considerations arise. Based on these you can decide which language you should use to implement your program. Of course, the majority of your decision is limited by your own knowledge of languages. Many of us are familiar with maybe four or five different programming languages, but in actual practice, we usually use only one or two of the languages on a given project.

Now it may be that for different stages in the project you'll utilize different languages. For instance, you may need to develop a prototype, in which case what you're looking for in a language may at this stage be completely different than what is demanded from the final, shipping version of the program. For a prototype, as was mentioned earlier, the primary capability you need from a language is flexibility: the capability of the language to easily and rapidly make changes to the prototype as needed.

For Windows programmers one of the best recent additions to our arsenal of languages has been Microsoft's Visual Basic program. It is a wonderful prototyping tool we've utilized for developing and testing interfaces. Its graphical design capabilities and direct links between the visual elements and the code provided a perfect foundation for quickly developing functional prototypes of various features in the programs we've developed. And with a lot less effort than would be required had we coded the prototypes in C++, we were able to easily manipulate the code to reflect desired changes to the interface.

Of course, Visual Basic isn't limited to producing prototypes alone. Many fine programs are available which have been developed with this language. With its superb support for custom controls, a unique community of developers specializing in Visual Basic has formed. It is a language that has become widely used in corporate computing environments, primarily because of its flexibility, its ease of use, and accessibility to databases.

At Borland, one of the by-products of a gargantuan effort put into the development of a foundation class-library that became the basis for Quattro Pro for Windows was an excellent graphic-design subsystem. With it we were able to design and develop the dialog boxes needed by the program, as well as provide for the users the capability of creating their own dialog boxes.

Modeled after the NeXT machine's beautiful Interface Builder, we could pick from a palette of interface elements—like group boxes, radio buttons, listboxes, and so on—and place them on the screen, automatically align them, and indicate any actions that could be performed when the element was activated. Because we had developed this in C++, we were able to utilize the object-oriented nature of the language to surface an object's methods, its "verbs," for use by other objects, and by the program as a whole. This allowed us to develop an entire subsystem of command objects—originally designed as a means of providing for the macro programming functionality that is a staple of spreadsheet software—that could be accessed and utilized by other parts of the program. It is through these command objects that we were able to link the graphic design elements with actions that could be performed.

This graphic-design subsystem not only gave us the ability to develop the dialog boxes—and even the toolbars, which were a specialized type of dialog box—that were a part of the program's interface, we also were able to provide the end users with the ability to easily construct their own additions to the program. With this, they could build their own programs for handing various things, like order entry, customer tracking, accounts payable maintenance, and the like. Because of the richness of its capabilities, many things could easily and quickly be developed utilizing this interface subsystem.

With this subsystem we were able to turn C++ into a prototyping language, and therefore use the prototype as a foundation for the final version of the programs that would be developed. We were able to gain the most from the demands of a prototyping language as well as the demands from a final development language from the same code base. And because we were utilizing an object-oriented language, we were able to add to the capabilities of the whole system as we used it for developing our prototypes. Various interface elements—like custom date controls, for instance—were created and added to the system to later be used by other parts of the program.

In some cases you will encounter, it may be that a language you are unfamiliar with is best suited for the task at hand. This must weigh in as one of your criteria for choosing the language you're going to use to implement the program. When it comes to using languages you aren't proficient with yet, the first consideration is how long do you have to develop the program? If you're under a tight, rock-solid schedule, you won't have the luxury of learning a new language. Therefore, what may be the best language—either for technical or practical reasons, or both—in fact turns out to be the worst development language for the task. If, on the other hand, you have the flexibility of being able to learn a new language, take advantage of it.

Learning a new language increases your development capabilities. Sometimes you'll need to take the initiative and learn the language on your own. Other times your employer may see the benefit of having you learn the new language and passing it on to others in the organization. Regardless of the case, one of the strongest recommendations we can make is to take the effort to learn new languages or methodologies whenever you can, for with them you are increasing the tools you can use for developing programs later on down the line. With them you have at your disposal the ability to choose from a wide array of languages that can be used to solve the various tasks of which a program is composed.

This isn't to say, however, that multiple languages are simultaneously used in the development of a program. As was mentioned earlier, it's been our experience that usually C and/or C++ along with assembly language are what we've used—and what most people in the commercial software development community have used—to construct programs. Again, the stages of the project may require the use of different languages—Visual Basic for prototyping; C++ for the bulk of development; assembly language modules for highly optimized code, and code that needs to communicate directly with the operating system. It hasn't been our experience—nor anyone else's we've encountered so far—to use, say, Modula-2, C, and ADA together at the same time to develop a program. These can be used together—there may well be a reason to do this—but typically, as we've encountered in our experiences, the choice of languages is limited to a small set of languages that can easily be used together to construct a program.

Algorithms

One of the most important aspects in software development is the choice of algorithms used to implement the program. Selection of the algorithm used to solve a given task is something that should be carefully considered, because a wrong selection and subsequent implementation could be costly in both time and energy. It is our intention here to give you some of the insights we've gained in the process of selecting an algorithm for implementing a task, but not to provide a detailed examination of the design and development of algorithms. There are many fine computer science books available that examine this aspect of algorithms in more detail than is possible in the scope of this book.

As with many other aspects of software development, one of the best things you can do is to have at your disposal references and resources you can utilize in your search for the "right" algorithm. We enclosed the term "right" with quotes because there is a subjective quality that any algorithm has. As with the selection of programming languages, what is right for any given situation is based on the demands and various aspects of the task at hand.

When selecting an algorithm, you'll be weighing such things as efficiency and benefits in execution speed against the complexity and time involved in implementing the algorithm in code. What may be the perfect algorithm, in a technical sense, may be the wrong algorithm because it will take too long to code. This may sound heretical for a developer to say, because the search for the best algorithm—with little or no regard for the complexity in implementing it in code—was one of the founding principles of our computer science education. But what is important in an academic situation may not be applicable in the business world, where time is money and money is the yardstick by which the company is judged. Unfortunately, in the very competitive world of commercial software development, there often isn't enough time to properly do the research necessary for finding the technically best algorithm.

This doesn't mean, however, that algorithm selection is brushed aside, or taken lightly. It is just that the techniques we used in college have in practice changed due to the circumstances. We have learned that just as it's important to build a library of reusable code and reference materials that can be utilized to implement code, it's just as important to build a library of algorithms and references of algorithms that are readily handy when an algorithm selection must be made.

Having had an education in computer science, we have at our disposal various text books with generalized algorithms that provide a foundation for our selection process. If you didn't study computer science in college, or you traded your books in after you were done with them, think about getting some of these basic algorithm books and putting them into your library. Many of the essential algorithms—for handling things like searching, ordered lists, database file manipulations, and the like—are contained in these books. And many implement their algorithms in a pseudocode syntax that easily can be implemented in whatever code you're using to develop the program. If you'd prefer taking an economical approach to this, you can utilize your local library's reference materials for this purpose. Of course, you may not have the luxury of taking the book with you, for if it's in the reference section you probably won't be able to check out the book. And if it's in the general circulation section, you run the risk of not being able to access the book because it's already been checked out by someone else. We highly suggest keeping at least one or two books detailing algorithms in your personal library. If you're economy-minded, you usually can pick up used books from a local college bookstore, or even from a friend or coworker for that matter.

Other excellent reference materials to have at your disposal are the various programmer's journals and magazines that are available. Some are generalized overviews of programming and algorithm design; others are specialized to programming languages—like C and C++, for example—or to platforms—like Macintosh, or Windows and DOS. Some journals are devoted to a specific niche of program development, like the development of business applications within the corporate environment. These various journals and magazines often provide algorithms for specific situations—like utilizing Julian dates, for instance—and often include implementations in a common high-level language, like C.

There are also on-line reference materials available for most of the common platforms. In the past couple of years, algorithms and code examples have been published on CD-ROM by Microsoft (for the IBM PC-compatible platform) and Apple (for the Macintosh platform) with a multitude of information at your disposal. These are also invaluable tools to have because the storage capabilities and small size of the CD-ROM medium provide for an enormous amount of information that can easily and readily be accessed for a reasonable price, when compared against hard-copy versions of the same information. So if you have a CD-ROM drive, you should carefully consider adding a CD-ROM-based collection of reference materials to your library. We've found it extremely handy to be able to pop a disc into the CD-ROM drive, search a subject, and in a matter of seconds have a list of topics relating to the subject we're interested in. And often, within a matter of minutes, a simple solution to a rather complex problem has been found, with an incredible savings in time and energy.

Other electronic sources that can be utilized in your algorithm selection process are the various on-line services available. Many of the services—like CompuServe and America Online—have areas, or forums, devoted to specific programming topics. Within these forums you can find libraries with samples of code that may implement something you need. In most cases there is a section within the forum for posting messages with questions about how to solve a given problem. Other members of the forum can post replies to the questions you post, sometimes with amazing insights and in an incredibly short amount of time. Usually, though, it takes a few days for responses to trickle in, so if you're in a big hurry to get an answer, this may not be the best method. But if you indicate in the subject that there is an urgency to the message—like prefacing the subject with URGENT!—you'll usually get results quicker.

The great thing about these forums is that you're a member of what's commonly being called a *virtual community* these days, a community not limited by time or geography, a community of people with common desires and insights sharing their experiences and helping one another. It's difficult to express the feeling of posting a question that maybe you've agonized about, found so difficult to solve, and someone replies they'd run into the same problem not too long ago and here's how it was solved. It's also very rewarding to help others out with the things you've learned as well.

Again, as with other aspects of the development of your software, utilizing other teammates, friends, and professional contacts is likewise invaluable. Talking about your solutions with others is something that should be used whenever possible. It may be difficult to find the time to do this, either because you're so busy doing your own stuff, or because it's difficult to interrupt others. There are other, non-interruptive ways of discussing algorithms and solutions that can be used. During the long hours we spent developing the Norton Desktop for Windows, for instance, we would take an hour or so out for dinner—usually pizza and sodas (thanks, Symantec!)—and during this time we would go over problems we were having. It was an efficient means of informally reviewing and solving problems each of us encountered. We weren't imposing on each other, nor were we causing a delay in implementing our own tasks.

Of course, these dinner discussions weren't the only times we spent reviewing problems and solutions. We often would call each other, or stop by each other's office and go over stuff. But these were, for efficiency reasons, limited to specific, usually urgent situations, because of the time constraints we all were under. For the most part, we utilized our e-mail system to pose questions to one another. If you've got e-mail within your organization, use it! There are many e-mail systems available that make it possible to send messages to a specific group of people—say Macintosh programmers, for example. It's an incredibly efficient means of solving problems with little or no imposition or interruption of other team members.

The selection of an algorithm you'll be using to implement a task in your program can be aided by maintaining the algorithms you've utilized in the past and keeping at your disposal various reference materials and resources that can be used when necessary. The biggest hindrance to selecting the best algorithm, at least in the experiences we've had in developing commercial software, is taking the time to do the research. If you can cut down the amount of research time, you'll be increasing your ability to access and use a wide variety of algorithms for implementing your code. It's like each bit of knowledge you have within your reach is a new color that can be used alone, or combined with other "colors" to paint new pictures, to construct new solutions to the tasks we encounter each time we develop a program.

Of course, if you're a consultant—or change companies often—it may be difficult for you to build an algorithm library because often the company you are working for owns just about every aspect of the software you create. Obviously it's not prudent to take whole sections of code from one company to another. And if there's a rather unique algorithm that was designed within the company, it wouldn't be too smart to share that with another company. It's probably best to build your algorithm library from publically available sources such as computer science journals and programming magazines.

The Development Environment

Because a large amount of our time as developers is spent coding and debugging the code we've written, the environment in which we develop is an important part of our overall working experience. It can have a positive or a negative impact on our productivity, on our feelings about the project we're working on, and viewpoints of ourselves as individuals and programmers. If the development environment is helping us do our job more effectively, we ultimately will feel better about what we're doing, and about ourselves. If, on the other hand, the development environment gets in our way and causes frustrations, these frustrations will be carried over and sometimes be amplified in other aspects of our lives, in our outlook of the project, and our own selves.

Although it is beyond the scope of this book to go into a detailed examination of the various development environments that are available, we'd instead like to again provide for you some of the experiences we've encountered—both pleasant and unpleasant—in the development environments we've worked in.

When it comes to the various pieces of your development environment, the tools you'll be using, it's best to do your own research and determine what your own needs and expectations from the environment are. Using these criteria, you can choose the best tools that supply you with the best development environment. As with other software tools, checking in recent issues of developer's magazines is a good way of determining which tools are best for you.

In general, it's been our experience that the development environment consists of the following major components:

- The computer

- The operating system

- The text editing software

- Reference materials

- The compiler and debugger

- Project management and version control

We'll be examining each of these in more detail in the following sections.

The Computer

The choice of computer system you use for developing your program is important. Ideally, you want the fastest, easiest, best equipped, and most economical system available. There often is a tradeoff between getting the most technically capable system and its price. If you have no budget considerations—say you're working for a company that is more concerned with having the best systems available for its developers than keeping down capital expenses (which is a luxury, believe us!)—then take advantage of it and get the fastest, highest-end system available. As is usually the case, though, you'll need to weigh the overall value of a system, and get the best system you can for the least amount of money.

The first consideration is the basic system itself. What platform are you developing for? You obviously won't be using an Intel-based computer to develop Macintosh applications. You'll be looking for the best system—the fastest processor, bus, and so forth—for the platform you'll be developing for. When considering the purchase of a system, and when you need to be value-oriented, often the most economical approach is to go not with the latest processor, but with the processor the latest one replaces. For instance, at the time of this writing, Intel's Pentium chip is the latest, fastest chip available for the Intel-based platform. It replaces the i486, which now is considerably cheaper than when it was the leading-edge chip a few years ago. You may feel, however, that the purchase of a Pentium-based system is in the long run a better, more economical system that meets your needs.

If you've already got a system, with each new project you begin you have an opportunity to take the time to reevaluate your system and see how it can be enhanced for your benefit. Maybe you're currently using a 33 MHz 486-based system, for example. Because of the price reductions in the more advanced chips, it may be economical to simply upgrade the chip to a faster version of the 486, or perhaps put in a new Pentium-based motherboard.

Once you've got the basic system, you need to see what your needs are for storage, display, and other capabilities. As with the basic system itself, you want the most bang for your buck. If you're going to be developing multimedia applications, your storage requirements are significantly more intensive than if you're developing shareware utilities, for example. And your requirements for your display probably will be higher as well. Just as in choosing the language you'll be using to develop the program, the demands of the tasks at hand should be used to determine the needs you have for your computer system.

When it comes to the display, special mention should be made to development within graphical operating systems. It's been our experience that the better capabilities your display has—both the display card and monitor—the happier you're going to be in the long run. For various considerations, primarily ergonomic, you should cut corners elsewhere in the system before you pinch bucks off your display system. The impact it can have on your productivity and effectiveness as a programmer is something we've experienced first-hand. Waiting for the display to update when scrolling in Windows is enough to make any programmer flinch. Its negative impact on visual stamina was noticed as well. The better the quality of the electronic display system, the less impact it will have on straining your own biological optical system.

When it comes to peripherals, your needs may be based on the project you're developing. Obviously, if you're developing multimedia software, you'll need capabilities for playing and recording sound, perhaps music, maybe access to data on a CD-ROM drive. Regardless of your needs for peripherals, one thing highly recommended is backup storage. Through the experience of handling Technical Support at Peter Norton Computing, many stories were told of people who lost all their data—sometimes irretrievably—and who didn't have backups of that data. If you don't currently have a backup system, preferably a hardware-based one—like a tape-backup—do yourself a favor and get it now.

The Operating System

Just like the hardware system itself, the operating system you will be developing for is usually the operating system you'll be developing under as well. The choices for operating systems are more limited compared to hardware, yet can be an important consideration, especially in the Intel-based platform universe. Specifically, if you're developing for Windows, it may be that the tools you have (or you are familiar with) are DOS-based programs. There was a time when this is all that was available. So the question became whether or not to develop within Windows itself, or simply to use Windows when you wanted to run the program you were writing. Until fairly recently (in Windows version 3.1), this was an important consideration, because it was fairly easy to bring the whole system to its knees, with the potential of losing data—usually code—you'd been working on in the process. Now, though, this is less of a concern because of safety enhancements to the latest version of Windows, and because of the Windows-hosted development tools now available.

The Text Editing Software

The software we developers use to write the code for our programs is often like a foreign language. Once you're comfortable with using it, with its features and capabilities, it's difficult to learn a new one. Like a language, situations sometimes arise in which we have to learn a new text editor. Making the shift from DOS to Windows, or from Windows to the Macintosh, is like moving to a new country with a different language. In order to function in that new culture, you've got to learn a few new tricks.

What we've found important for the text editors we use is how easy it is to use or to learn new things, and how expandable it is. Some features like column manipulations and macro recording capabilities are invaluable tools once you've used them. You notice it when they're not available.

The features and capabilities and how easy it is to use the software are things you'll have to determine on your own, using your own individual criteria. All we can say is it has been our experience that a great deal of our time has been spent using our text editors, so taking the time to find the one you're most comfortable with is extremely important.

Reference Materials

In numerous places we've mentioned the importance of having additional resources readily available. The most efficient are on-line resources. Having technical manuals, books, and articles available and within easy electronic reach is something not to be missed. The amount of time saved doing an automated lookup or search for a topic is incredible. Sometimes, it may be more comfortable to use the hard copy manual, so you may want to keep them around as well.

In addition to on-line reference materials, we've also found it indispensable to have our address books and calendars digital as well. When you've got a question you need to call a friend about, having the number available electronically is really handy. And if you've got access to an electronic organizer or personal digital assistant (PDA)—preferably one you can connect to your desktop computer—you've also got the capability of keeping that information handy with you at all times, just like with a paper-based address book and calendar.

The Compiler and Debugger

Your compiler is your workhorse. It churns out the code that becomes the program your end user utilizes. You want a compiler that is quick, produces efficient and safe code, and is easy to set up and use. In our experiences we've only used compilers by major language tools vendors, such as Microsoft, Symantec, and Borland, mainly because that is what was standardized. There are many fine compilers available for various platforms and operating systems, so choosing the best one for your situation is something you need to research.

One interesting aspect of having worked at Borland is that we had access to the tools developed by the languages staff. This was a dual-edged sword. On one hand, we were able to request enhancements to the tools—to fine-tune them to our liking—that weren't available to the public at large. Most of these enhancements found their way into future, shipping versions of the tools. This was an extremely useful aspect of working for Borland, for we were able to more easily construct our software than if we had to rely on limitations in the currently available set of tools.

On the other hand, the downside to this was we were often guinea pigs testing new programs. Sometimes development of our own programs was impeded because of bugs in the tools; but these occasions were few and far between—and the effort the members of the languages staff put into their products on our behalf is and always will be greatly appreciated.

An important adjunct to your compiler is your debugger. Enough can't be said about using a debugger. Doing a unit test by stepping through the code you've just written is a valuable technique for catching bugs before much time goes by. The quicker you can catch bugs, the better off you're going to be. When looking at debuggers, you want something that's going to provide the best means of allowing you to quickly discover bugs, the reason for the bugs, and therefore solutions to the bugs. And something that automatically checks certain things for you—like whether you're writing data out of bounds—is extremely useful, especially when trying to track down those deep, hidden, difficult-to-find bugs.

Project Management and Version Control

Typically most of the software projects we've been involved with have demanded that a large number of source files be created and therefore managed. Being able to keep track of all of these files and how they fit into the overall program is an indispensable tool. It is further enhanced when file management is tied in with the version control system.

Project management software is also capable of determining the dependencies individual components of the project have on one another. So when you make modifications to a header file—say you've added a new virtual method, for instance—the source modules that include that header file need to be recompiled. Having this automated is a valuable way of recompiling only those files that need to be recompiled, and not just doing a full rebuild every time a modification is made.

Often enhancements are available to the components of your development system that can be used in conjunction with your version control system. Some text editors, for instance, have the ability to handle the checking in and checking out of source code modules from the version control system.

To wrap things up, there has been a tendency over the past several years to integrate the development environment. Much can be said in favor of this, primarily savings in cost as compared with buying the components individually, a savings in the amount of hard disk space allocated to the integrated environment as opposed to individual components, and the level of integration available among the individual pieces of the integrated environment that may not be possible when individual dissimilar programs are used.

There is a new tendency, however, in which the integrated environments are being opened up so the individual components of the integrated system can be replaced with existing, outside components. This provides the best of both worlds, an environment in which the power of integrating the components can be combined with the richness and specificity available in outside components. If you don't like the text editor that comes with the integrated package, you can replace it with one you like better, but in a seamless manner, with full access to the rest of the integrated system, as if the manufacturer of the integrated environment had licensed your text editor and adapted it to fit in the integrated system.

Safe Programming

Ideally, as programmers we'd like to write bug-free code. One of the best ways to avoid bugs in your software is to try and catch them before they appear, and one of the best ways to accomplish this is to program defensively. We'll briefly go over some of the tricks and techniques we've learned that squashed the bugs before they had a chance to crawl into the hidden areas of the program.

One of the first things to do is to declare a variable, then initialize it immediately, preferably on the same line on which you're declaring the variable. Before we started using this technique with almost religious fervor, we can't tell you the number of times we spent valuable time tracking down a bug caused by an uninitialized variable. By declaring and then immediately initializing your variables, you'll be rid of a major cause of software bugs.

Some variables aren't easy or convenient to initialize at the same time they're being declared. Character arrays and structures are examples of this. So if it's not convenient to immediately initialize a variable, get into the habit of initializing them as soon as possible in the code, preferably right after the block of code where your variables are declared.

This C++ code is an example of what we're talking about:

```
//------------------------------------------------------
//                                          PaintCaption
//------------------------------------------------------
BOOL PaintCaption ()
{
    BYTE        szTempStr [maxTempStrLen + 1];
    RECT        rcTextBox;
    int         nStrLen = 0;
    memset (szTempStr, '\0', maxTempStrLen);
    SetRectEmpty (&rcTextBox);
    // .. the rest of the code....
    return TRUE;
}
```

In the above example, the character array and Rect structure are initialized as one of the first things in the program. Note the integer nStrLen is initialized immediately upon declaration. You'd be surprised the amount of time you can save by doing this simple thing.

If you're utilizing an object-oriented language, like C++, you can embed initialization of your objects within the structures and classes themselves. (If you're unfamiliar with C++, classes are essentially the same thing as structures, but encapsulate both data members and functions. The data and functions can be hidden from use by other objects in the program. In C++, structures are classes, only all of their data members and methods are public, that is, they're readily visible and available to other objects in the program.)

For example, one of our favorite Windows tricks is to take existing Windows structures and wrap them in a C++ wrapper. The Rect structure we used above can be initialized automatically by doing the following:

```
//----------------------------------------------------
// This is a wrapper for Windows' RECT structure and
// provides a means of automatically initializing the
// object when it is created.
//----------------------------------------------------
struct Rect : public RECT
{
        // Default constructor:
        //
    Rect ()
        {
        SetRectEmpty ((LPRECT) this);
        }
    // .. rest of the structure...
};
```

Each time a new variable of type Rect is created or declared, its constructor will be called, and therefore the call initializes the members of the object.

For those objects you create on your own, you can take this technique and apply it to the object itself. We like to use an InitMembers() method that is called by the constructor(s) in the object and serves the purpose of initializing all of the data members that are in the object.

For instance, say you've got an object that is a displayable rectangle, that has as its attributes a display context (a "DC" in Windows parlance), a display style, and a color. Here's how you can automatically initialize the object when it is created:

```
//----------------------------------------------------
// This is a displayable rectangle and demonstrates
// how to automatically initialize the object when it
// is created.
//----------------------------------------------------
class DisplayRect : public Rect
{
    protected:
            HDC             theDC;
            COLORREF        theColor;
            RectStyle       theStyle;    // An enumeration
                                         ➡defined
                                         // elsewhere.

    public:
            DisplayRect ()
```

```
                    {
                    InitMembers();
                    }
            DisplayRect (HDC dc)
                    {
                    InitMembers ();
                    theDC = dc;
                    }
            void InitMembers()
                    {
                    theDC       = NULL;
                    theColor    = RGB (0,0,0);
                    theStyle    = plainRectStyle;
                    }
    };
```

As you can see in the above example, we've placed the function decla-
rations inline in the header file. In practice, we'll often place the con-
structors and the member initializer methods into the source file. By
doing this we save time so that when we need to make modifications
to the object we're not always updating the header file, that in some
cases may cause a lengthy recompilation of the program.

When you're creating dependents of objects, note that when the constructor for the base class is invoked, the InitMembers() method for the
base object is called as well, so the base object's data members are initialized. This is a really useful way of ensuring that you're initializing
your objects properly when they're being created.

Sometimes simple text editing tricks can keep bugs out of your way.
Take the switch statement, for instance. There have been a few occasions when we've quickly coded something and forgotten to include
a break at the end of a case construct. This causes an unwanted fall-
through from one case construct to the following one. It's a simple
enough bug to find, but still rather time-consuming when it's so easy
to get into the habit of immediately adding the break at the end of
each case construct you type in.

Another simple switch statement habit to get into is to always include
a default statement at the end of the switch statement. There are occasions when the default statement shouldn't ever be reached, and this is
an easy way of indicating that an error condition has been reached.

One of the most powerful error trapping techniques is to utilize an
assert() function for testing the validity of a given situation. The
power of the assert() function is that during development it can spit

out useful debugging error information, and can be turned off in the final version of the program, so it's not visible to the end user.

As a final example of defensive programming, one of the most common and sometimes one of the most difficult bugs we've encountered is a memory overwrite bug. This occurs when your program goes off willy-nilly writing into areas it isn't supposed to, often with disastrous results. Many overwrite bugs are only encountered under unusual, sometimes irreproducible circumstances, because the area that's being overwritten may contain important data that's being used by the program.

So how do you avoid memory overwrite bugs? Well, we've taken the right first step by initializing our variables when we declare them. For example, when a variable we're using to set the upper bounds of a sequential operation isn't initialized properly, our program may go beyond the boundary and write into areas it's not supposed to.

Some memory overwrites are caused by a discrepancy in the size of a structure in different object files. Consider what happens when you have declared a structure in a header file, and that header is shared among numerous modules. Say you've used this structure in your program for a while and later decide to remove a member or two from it. If you fail to recompile all of the modules that depend on that header, you are in for trouble.

These modules will assume that the structure has more room than it really does and will attempt to read or—worse still—write beyond the actual end of it. Some other data, or even program code, may inadvertently get overwritten. It almost is a guarantee for a crash to happen.

The bad news is that a bug like this is very difficult to track down. The crash usually does not occur immediately, only after some other function encounters the corrupted data. It can take you several hours with the debugger to find out that the crash was really caused by a memory overwrite that took place much earlier.

The good news is that you can prevent the problem by making use of the automatic dependency checking mechanism. Traditionally, a MAKE utility is used for that purpose, but modern development environments provide the equivalent functionality via project management facilities. If you are not using any of these, why not?

When you add a new data member to—or remove an existing one from—a structure, you'll need to recompile all the modules using that structure to maintain consistency throughout your program. Also, in C++, when you manipulate any of the virtual methods—by adding, removing, or reordering them—you'll likewise need to recompile those modules using the modified class.

Finally, when it comes to programming, try to anticipate what problems each of your functions and methods may encounter and accommodate for them. Think of what the boundary conditions are and put in code to handle them. Is an input value valid, is it within its expected lower and upper range? And when you're using pointers to data, take the time to test the validity of the object before you use it. In most cases it's a small amount of code to put in that can ensure you'll never be referencing a NULL pointer, for instance.

Debugging

While it seems apparent that debugging is an essential part of the development process, you'd be surprised at the number of developers we've met who only do a cursory debugging job. They typically use their debuggers in a reactionary manner, in response to a bug that's been reported. One of the things we've found to be an invaluable adjunct to defensive programming is utilizing your debugging software in an offensive manner: take the time to look for bugs before they crop up.

One of the easiest ways to accomplish this is to do a unit test on each function soon after it's been created. Go into the debugger and step through the function and make sure it does what it's expected to do, the first time through. Then go back and see what happens when a lower or upper boundary condition is met, then exceeded. Then see what happens when you send in junk to the function. If your code performs well under these circumstances, chances are it'll work in the real world as well.

As was mentioned earlier, debugging programs are available to trap things such as memory overwrites for you automatically. We highly recommend adding these kinds of tools to your arsenal because when it comes to debugging, you're going to need all the help you can get. There's so much complexity to the software we write, and we're writing it under such time pressure that often it's difficult to anticipate most of the extreme conditions that can be encountered when the program is actually run. By having an extra hand in there looking at the program for you, you can concentrate on those areas of debugging that are not as easily automated and require human ingenuity to solve.

As a final note about debugging, there are some circumstances where it's really helpful to have a teammate or a friend sitting with you as you're going through and debugging the program. There have been several instances where we've encountered bugs that seemed to have no root, that just couldn't be tracked down. Many times, by working through the problem with someone else, you're able to utilize his or her insights and experiences to overcome a difficult-to-solve problem. Perhaps the other person has run into a bug like this before and knows what to look for. It can make the debugging process significantly easier when more than one mind is being used.

Staying Productive

If you're a programmer, you've more than likely had times where you've spent long hours developing your code. This is typically the case when deadlines arise and need to be met, especially in the later stages of the project. During these times you need to focus on staying as productive as possible, even under extreme circumstances. We've run into this situation more than a few times ourselves and have a few pointers on making it through the rough times.

Office Environment

We all know we spend a significant amount of time at our place of employment. You need to ensure your environment is as enjoyable and as close to your liking as possible to maintain your stamina and productivity.

We've worked places where we had cubicles and places where we had private offices. Both environments have their pros and cons, but it's been our experience that the ability to shut a door and tune out the world and concentrate on the task at hand is not a luxury but at times a necessity. If you're in a cubicle situation, we've found music and headphones to be an indispensable tool in drowning out the world when necessary.

Regardless of your situation, you need to be sure you're as comfortable as possible. A high quality chair and compatible desk are essential for staying comfortable, especially during marathon programming sessions. For your chair, make sure your back is being supported in the most proper manner; for your desk, you want to make sure it's at the proper height for you, that when you're typing on the keyboard it's in a comfortable position. It's usually best if your monitor is in a comfort-able viewing position for you, and that it's at the proper viewing dis-tance. If you've got the capability of accessing someone with either environmental, ergonomic, or occupational therapy experience, utilize his or her talents to make sure you're got the best possible working environment.

Lighting is another important aspect of your environment. Often the aspects of lighting—the type of lighting (incandescent, halogen, or fluorescent) and how bright the lighting is—are subjective qualities that differ from one individual to the next. With private offices, the individual's control over his or her lighting is usually easily handled. For cubicle situations, however, it may be a little more difficult. In those open spaces it may be possible to group together people with similar lighting desires. For instance, all those who like the fluorescent bulbs in the typical office environment can go in one area, all those who like more subdued, less bright halogen lighting in another area, and so on. In this way the needs of the individual and the organization as a whole can be combined.

It's also important that your work environment have a kitchen because you need to drink and eat something on occasion. OK, we've had situ-ations where eating and drinking are unfortunate necessities, but they are necessities nonetheless. If you've got someplace within your envi-ronment you can go to get sustenance, it's going to make your life a lot simpler than if you have to go to a roach coach or an outside restau-rant. We've found it convenient to bring a few snacks to work each day and keep them at our desk for when we want something. Fruit and trail mixes are pretty popular, at least as far as we've encountered.

Another important aspect of your work environment is keeping fun things within easy reach. Hey, we spend enough time being serious about what we do; it's really important to let loose, even in a simple manner, on occasion. Many of the people we've had the pleasure of working with have kept toys readily available, especially during those extended compile times. Getting into limited exchanges with those toy foam weapons is a great way to blow off a little steam without causing much damage—either to property or to one another.

For those times when you need to put in huge amounts of overtime, maybe it would be wise to keep a sleeping bag, or a pillow and blanket handy so you don't feel you have to drive home in the wee hours of the morning and risk falling asleep at the wheel. Some of the places we've worked have had a couch available for just this purpose.

Whatever you can do to improve the way you feel about being at work, do it. Take some time and think about it. If you're feeling stressed, see if there isn't something that can be changed in your environment to keep you relaxed a bit more. Maybe it's as simple as cleaning your desk; maybe it's getting and tending for another plant. Perhaps it's a drastic change, like getting a better chair or monitor. Whatever can be done to make your time at work more enjoyable will in the long run more than pay for any incurred costs—especially during those crunch times when long hours are the norm.

Taking Breaks

One of the goals of marathon programming is staying productive—being able to function properly—under extreme circumstances. Just like a long-distance runner, you need to pace yourself if you are going to finish the race and complete the program on time. Stepping away from the desk on occasion isn't a waste of time, but instead an investment in your future. Because, like it or not, it's just not feasible for us to remain chained to our desks in front of our monitors for hours and hours on end. We need to step away and recharge ourselves occasionally.

A little trick an ophthalmologist said once is to take a large glass to work, preferably 32 ounces or larger. Every hour or so, go to the lunch room and fill the glass with (hopefully bottled) water and gradually drink it as you're doing your work. Not only are you meeting your nutritional needs of pumping fluids into your system, you're also forcing yourself to step away from the computer for at least a little while. And because you're drinking a large amount of water, you'll also be required to take another break and head for the bathroom. This really ends up forcing you to rest your eyes on occasion. It also has the added benefit of forcing you to get up out of your chair and stretch your legs and use some of your muscles in a different manner.

As a final note about taking breaks, don't feel shy about kicking your feet up on the desk, closing your eyes, listening to music, and completely tuning out the world. Sometimes during a lengthy compile this is a great way of catnapping and re-energizing yourself for the long hours ahead of you. If you're familiar with meditation techniques, or more comfortable praying, utilize it for your benefit. It's not who stays up the longest, it's who's able to get the most done that truly matters. Use whatever it takes to do this, including falling asleep from time to time.

Knowing When to Quit

During marathon programming sessions it's sometimes difficult to know when to back off, when to scale back and take some time for recuperation. There comes a point when no matter what we do, we're either too tired or too stretched to perform efficiently. If we monitor ourselves for these situations, we'll know that we're not performing at our peak and it's time to think about stopping, at least for a while.

We've been in situations where we simply just had to stay up for extended periods of time, usually to get a beta copy of the program out the door by a certain time. These have been circumstances in which we just had to do it, no matter how tough, no matter how unproductive we truly were.

But fortunately, these circumstances are rare, so when you're in a situation where you can stop, it is highly recommended that you do so. Even if you get away for just a short time, you'll probably find that when you come back you'll be able to get more accomplished than if you'd stayed and worked on through.

We've also noticed a tendency among ourselves and people in the commercial software development industry as a whole not to take vacations. Sometimes the circumstances of product schedules don't readily allow for us taking vacations. This is usually because we're either busily developing a program, or have just completed one and need to be around in case problems arise. While this sometimes is an understandable necessity, when you're between projects, take the time to completely get away from it all and relax. You deserve it, you need it, and it's going to do you lots of good over the long haul.

In conclusion, no matter what the demands of your development environment may be, you have a primary responsibility to take care of yourself so you are able to maximize your productivity without burning yourself out. If you feel like you're stressed, figure out what it would take to reduce, or hopefully eliminate the stress. There have been numerous recent medical investigations linking health difficulties to stress. Eat properly, get some exercise, have outside interests that don't involve computers, and make sure you feel good about yourself. In the end you'll find your ability to perform your duties as a programmer will be increased.

Conclusion

In this chapter we've seen the ways in which the product code is implemented:

- A schedule is used to discern the features to be in the product and the resources available to work on these features.

- Before the implementation can begin, the language best suited for creating the program must be decided upon.

- Algorithms serve as the basic recipes of the program.

- Your development environment should be carefully designed.

- Continued productivity through difficult times can be accomplished by pacing yourself and taking care of yourself both physically and mentally.

Chapter 4

Benefiting from Object-Oriented Programming

Although object-oriented programming (OOP) has been around for well over 20 years now, it is not until fairly recently that OOP has entered the mainstream of the programming community. In this chapter we'll be taking a look at how we've utilized object-oriented programming at the companies we've worked for. We'll begin with an overview of the major concepts behind object-oriented programming:

- Object-oriented languages enable the programmer to bind data and the procedures meant to manage that data into a single element, the class.

- New classes can be created that are derived from other existing classes.

- The programmer can specify actions in derived classes that behave differently than those in the existing classes.

We'll then examine some of the benefits to be gained from OOP:

- Reusability of both data and code

- Enhanced ability to maintain existing code

- Cross-platform development

Finally, we'll conclude with how object-oriented programming has been used on some of the projects we've worked on.

It seems like it's only taken a few short years for the commercial software industry to embrace object-oriented programming (OOP) as the discipline of choice. Our first encounter with object-oriented programming was in early 1990 while at Peter Norton Computing. At that time the only commercially available full C++ compiler for the Intel platform was Zortech's product. It's now over four years later and not only are there are a number of OOP compilers available, but many of the products being developed are now written in C++.

In this chapter, we'll be taking a look at some of the things that we've encountered on our adventures in object-oriented programming. We'll begin by taking a brief look at some of the basic benefits of utilizing object-oriented programming. The remainder of the chapter will be devoted to recounting some of the experiences we've had in developing software using object-oriented methodologies.

Overview of the Benefits of Object-Oriented Programming

In this chapter, we assume that you already have a fundamental understanding of object orientation and are familiar with its terms and concepts. This overview is provided as a brief introduction for those readers unfamiliar with object orientation and its benefits. Experienced users of object-oriented methodologies can skip this section of the chapter.

An Overview of Object Orientation

Object orientation is an approach to software development where the emphasis is placed on the data a program is to deal with. It is an approach which has evolved from—and seeks to address specific problems with—the procedural approach to software development.

With procedural software development, an emphasis is placed on the subroutines—*functions* or *procedures*—in the program. Like object-oriented programming, the procedural approach evolved from and specifically aimed to solve problems with an earlier approach to programming. A major goal of procedural programming was to increase programmer productivity by clarifying the organization of a program. It aimed to bring a readily identifiable structure to a program by allowing the programmer to group code that accomplished a task within procedures.

In non-structured programming languages like BASIC (we're talking about early BASIC, not the more recent BASIC languages that are now procedural) the source code was typically very linear and flow through the program was mainly controlled by the GOTO statement. Although the programmer could group his or her code together into subroutines which could be accessed by the GOTO statement, there was little support of this concept in the language itself. Data within non-structured programs is typically globally available and provides little protection against errant modification of the data.

Procedural languages, like Pascal and C, specifically provide a means for the programmer to contain code in subunits within the program. They further provide a means for the programmer to group data within structures that can later be accessed as a single element. Not only does this provide a way for the developer to organize his or her data in the program, it provides a level of data security not available in non-structured languages.

Object-oriented languages are the next step in the evolution of programming languages. Although procedural languages are an improvement over their predecessors, there are a few ways in which object-oriented languages seek to improve upon procedural languages. First, they seek to bind data and procedures meant to manage that data into a single element. Second, they seek to provide a way for the programmer to reuse code and data in the objects which are created. Finally, they seek to allow the programmer a means of defining specialized actions for various objects.

Object-oriented languages seek to combine data structures and functions associated with these data structures into a single entity known as the *class*—which is a recipe for an object, which is an instance of a class. This element is often known as an *abstract data type* and provides two very powerful attributes: encapsulation and data hiding.

Encapsulation refers to the ability of the object-oriented language to bind a data type and its associated group of functions that operate on the data into a single object. *Data hiding*—also called *information hiding*—refers to a feature of object-oriented languages whereby access to the individual elements within the data type is protected. Access to both data members and functions—known as *methods*—is limited in object-oriented languages. It may be that some elements need to be generally available, or made *public*. Other elements of the object need to be hidden from users of the object, or made *private*. Further protection to the data is provided by limiting the scope of the object to avoid having to make data globally available.

Object-oriented languages also allow the programmer to create new objects that are based on other objects. This feature—called *inheritance*—means that code can be reused to construct new objects from all or part of an existing object. An object that is based on another class is said to be *derived* from the *base class*. *Multiple inheritance* means that an object is derived from more than one parent object. By building a hierarchy of base and derived classes—often called a *class library*—the programmer is able to create a code base which can be reused in many situations for a multitude of purposes. From a single implementation, the programmer is able to utilize the class library in many programs without the need for re-implementation in each program.

Closely connected to inheritance is the concept of *virtual methods*. With these specialized types of member functions, the programmer can specify that an action in a derived class be performed differently than that in the base class. For example, let's say you have a base class called Shape that is used to represent a geometric shape. Now Shape has a Draw() function that handles the output of Shape to a display device, like the monitor or printer. Let's say you've derived a couple of specialized Shapes, like Circle and Rectangle. You'll need a Draw() function for each of these derived objects, but you don't want to have to keep track of which Draw() function to call for each of the objects.

Well, that's where virtual functions come in, because in C++, for example, you can define the Draw() function with the *virtual* keyword in the Shape object and code a different implementation of Draw() in the Circle and Rectangle objects. When the Draw() function is called, the language knows which of the Draw() functions should be used based on the object itself. So, if you have a Circle and call the Draw() function, the language knows that you want Circle's Draw() function called, and not Shape's.

This is a very powerful feature because it frees the programmer from having to keep track manually of an object to know which function should be called. Without virtual functions, you'd have to identify the object somehow and, based on that, know which function needs to be invoked. Virtual functions ease the implementation of a reusable code base by automatically keeping track of this for you.

Now that we've briefly gone over the major attributes of object-oriented languages, let's take a look at some of the ways in which object orientation seeks to improve the development of software.

Object-oriented development aims to make the process of designing and implementing software quicker and easier than the procedural methods. One of the benefits of quicker and easier development is lower development costs. This is achieved by reusing data and code as much as possible. Further reductions in the overall cost of software development are achieved by easing the maintenance of software, by enhancing the reliability of a system, and by easing the transportability of software to differing platforms.

Reusability

As we saw above in the introductory overview, one of the major aspects of object-oriented languages is their support for the creation of reusable objects. What is the gain from reusing code?

Well, the first and perhaps most obvious gain is that you don't have to reinvent the wheel each time you need to construct a new vehicle. Let's say, for example, you've developed a program that's intended to be used by automobile designers as a means for them to test out new designs within the ease and flexibility of a computer environment.

Now, in your implementation you've got a Wheel object and have not only built several predefined specialized Wheel types, but also a means for the designer to create new wheels by establishing various attributes for the wheel. When the designer goes to add the Wheels to the car, he or she can pick from the predefined set of Wheels and directly put these on the car, or use these as the basis for a new type of Wheel. To make the system even more powerful, you allow the designer to save these newly created Wheels as if they were a part of the predefined set of Wheels. These newly created Wheels can themselves be used to create other new Wheels, which can be saved and used to create other new Wheels, and so on.

Through this, the automobile designer is spared the hassle of having to redesign the wheels for each new automobile. Likewise, by utilizing a set of objects, the software developer is spared the hassle of having to redesign, re-implement, and retest the objects in each new program. Very often a predefined set of objects are contained in class libraries that come with object-oriented compilers. The software developer can use these class library objects as a base for creating new objects, which can be used to create other new objects, and so forth.

So each time you don't have to redesign and re-implement something, you're saving yourself time and your employer money. The more data and code that can be reused, the easier and quicker the software will be to develop.

Maintainability

Another powerful aspect of object-oriented languages is the ability to enhance the maintainability of a program. Maintaining an existing program can be one of the most costly and difficult aspects of software development. By decreasing the difficulty of the maintenance effort, the amount of time involved and, hence, the cost of maintaining the code will likewise be decreased.

Object-oriented programming can aid in the maintenance of existing software by:

- Making sure additions and modifications to the source code don't end up breaking the program in other areas

- Making sure the code and its underlying logic are understandable and easy to modify

By utilizing features inherent in object-oriented programming languages, the software developer can enhance the maintainability of a program. Encapsulation and data hiding assist in software maintenance by allowing the programmer to make changes to a few select areas of the program. The implementation is protected by limiting access to the internals of the objects. So, changes to the software can be limited to select objects, which can be individually tested to ensure their reliability within the program.

Programs implemented in object-oriented languages tend to be more understandable by programmers because there is a direct link between the *problem domain* (why a program is needed) and the *solution domain* (how the program is implemented). From the problem domain, a clear definition of the objects, their actions, and attributes is obtained. From this, the classes, methods, and data members are defined and implemented in the solution domain, which is the program. In object-oriented software, the programmer is dealing with objects that are representations of the data the program is expected to handle. Understandability of the code is enhanced in object-oriented software because the objects, and the actions and attributes associated with these objects, are easily discernible.

Portability

One of the interesting benefits of object-oriented programming which has become apparent in the last few years is how it aids in the portability of software to both different operating systems and hardware platforms; we'll refer to this as a *run-time environment*.

As you'll see later in the chapter, object-oriented software development at the companies we've worked at has largely been used as a means of maximizing the portability of software. Portability has been enhanced at these companies through the creation of single-source class libraries which provide a foundation for the various run-time environments supported.

By utilizing the powers of object-oriented programming, generic interface objects (like windows, dialog boxes, buttons, and so on) can be created. These generic objects are implemented in specialized code for the various run-time environments. However, because these are generic objects, a single set of code can be written to use and manipulate these generic interface objects across the supported environments.

In this section we've taken a brief look at what object orientation is and some of its benefits. We've seen that the emphasis in object-oriented programming is on both the data and the process, as opposed to the procedures that deal with the data, as is the case in procedural languages. We've also seen that object-oriented languages provide direct support for encapsulation, data hiding, inheritance, and virtual functions. The section concluded with a look at some of the benefits of utilizing the powers of object-oriented programming.

In the next section, we'll be examining some of the experiences with object-oriented programming we've had at the companies we've worked for.

Early Encounters—Peter Norton Computing

Our encounter with object-oriented programming began in early 1990 when a few of us took a course in C++ programming at UCLA Extension. The course was a very well-organized, 10-week introduction to object-oriented programming in C++, taught by a research fellow from IBM with several years of C++ experience. We took the course primarily as a way of becoming familiar with an emerging discipline and to see if it was something we could utilize to develop our software. It isn't too difficult to say that we went into the course with a healthy dose of skepticism. It also isn't surprising that we came out of the course avid devotees of object-oriented programming. What proved to be difficult was to get others in the company to share our enthusiasm with the prospect of developing software utilizing object-oriented methodologies.

The Norton Library

One of the first things we encountered in learning to program in C++ was that it felt like this was a natural way to program, that the language's constructs supported the data abstraction and encapsulation we had begun to apply in our C programs. We were already approaching the development of the Norton Utilities and Norton Commander by basing the programs on a reusable code library. Unfortunately, each program was based on its own library, due mostly to historical reasons. The Utilities had been developed in-house, whereas the Norton Commander was originally developed by someone from outside the company. We were in the process of integrating the two libraries when we began the course at UCLA.

One of the projects we did for the course involved redesigning and redeveloping one of the modules for the Norton Commander. It proved not only to be a good exercise as far as the course was concerned, it also was a good exercise in moving existing code from C to C++.

The Norton Commander was a DOS program designed to augment and enhance the standard DOS shell. Users could easily navigate and access the directories and files on their system. The module from the Commander we chose to "port" was a dBASE file viewer. This program allowed the users to view the data in their dBASE files as if they were using dBASE itself, but with the speed and comfort of the Norton Commander.

From a design standpoint, the re-implementation was a fairly easy endeavor to accomplish, mainly because most of the data structures and functions were easily identifiable and, therefore, easily transportable to an object-oriented design. Because the design was relatively easy to port, the implementation was also fairly easy to accomplish.

We began the project by translating our existing data structures into classes, and attaching the functions to the objects they were associated with. This was, perhaps, the trickiest part of the port, mainly because object-oriented programming centers itself around the data that is to be utilized in the program. Procedural programming, on the other hand, is primarily concerned with the functions of the program. Some of the functions clearly belonged to a single object, whereas others could be attached to more than one object. In situations like this, we decided to rethink the purpose of the functions and see either if: 1) a new class needed to be designed that better fit the purpose of the pro-cedure; or, 2) if the functionality within the procedure could be broken apart and attached to the appropriate object.

One side effect of this exercise was that it gave the appearance that porting all of our existing code would be an easy undertaking. Unfortu-nately, this was not the case for a couple of reasons. The first is that each of the programs, the Utilities and the Commander, and their un-derlying libraries had been designed and developed by two very differ-ent programmers with very different design and programming styles. Neither was better than the other, just different, and therefore difficult to reconcile and combine into a single library and code base. Another problem was that the Utilities was a much older program than the Commander and, therefore, it had considerably more "baggage"—both from a design and implementation standpoint.

Both of these aspects of the two programs and their libraries pretty much meant that for any port into an object-oriented language to be successful—and to be done right—we would have to redesign and re-build from the ground up. In the world of commercial software devel-opment, taking the time and programming-power to accomplish this is at best difficult. In our case it proved to be impossible given our lim-ited development resources.

Although we could see a long-term benefit from undertaking the re-implementation of our libraries into a single object-oriented class library, we knew we didn't have the resources or the talent readily available to accomplish this task. It would entail a significant delay in the release of our products by diverting our development resources to the task. Many of the people in the organization, unfamiliar with object orientation, could not clearly ascertain the benefits of the task. It was therefore deemed too risky a project to undertake, and we took the quicker approach of combining the functionality of our existing libraries utilizing our current procedural programming scheme.

Looking back on it now, it seems rather unfortunate that we couldn't overcome the political difficulties and find the resources to build a team dedicated to the development of an object-oriented class library from which our future products could be based. The benefits of this would have meant that, down the line, our future products could more easily be developed by utilizing a common base of objects and code. But, at the time, there were few options available to us, and perhaps more significantly, a rather small talent pool to draw from.

Full Force Object Orientation—Symantec

Interestingly enough, a company we were only vaguely familiar with, but which would play a major role in our corporate lives later in the year, had already taken the plunge into object-oriented development. In fact, by early 1990, it was just beginning to undertake the strategy whereby all its future products would be based on a single, highly portable, object-oriented class library. The goal of the project was to simplify the development of its products and therefore shorten the time it took to develop these products.

That company is, of course, Symantec, that purchased Peter Norton Computing in mid-1990. One of the things that impressed us at Peter Norton was that the strategy Symantec took closely matched the way we would have undertaken the development of a class library had the resources been available. For one thing, a team dedicated solely to the purpose of developing and maintaining the class library was put together. Also, the team consisted of people specializing in the platform the class library was intended to support. But more importantly, it was a long-term development project, whose benefits would not become apparent right away, but later down the line.

Bedrock

Around the time Symantec purchased Peter Norton Computing, we were in the process of designing the Norton Desktop for Windows. As was explained earlier in the book, one of the first things Symantec did for our development group—what was known as "The Peter Norton Group"—was to make available any and all resources we needed to get the project done as soon as possible. This meant getting the people we needed to accomplish the tasks we had identified. It also meant getting a first-hand glimpse into something that had, until that point, been a rather secretive project.

The code-name of the project was Bedrock and it was the object-oriented, platform-independent class library that was to be the foundation of Symantec's future products. From our initial look at the project, we were rather impressed at what we saw. It appeared to be a fairly well-designed system with depth, especially given its platform independence. The particularly interesting aspects of the class library were its implementation of a platform independent user interface. This entailed not only a set of objects for windows, views, buttons, and the like, but also platform-independent resources. A single set of resources was developed for a product; each of the platforms Bedrock ran on utilized this same single set of resources. Dialogs, menus, icons, cursors, and other resources could be developed once and utilized by a single code base.

Between mid- and late-1989, we undertook an examination of what we wanted and needed as far as platform independence was concerned. We came to the conclusion that platform independence was primarily a user-interface issue, mainly because we were developing utility software. Utilities have traditionally been an augmentation to the operating system, so our approach to platform independence was to completely separate the user interface and the engine from each other. Again, because of limited development resources and product development time constraints we didn't have the opportunity to implement what we knew we wanted: a platform-independent user-interface class library.

The user-interface and single-set resource aspects of Bedrock were particularly appealing to us. If we could utilize the power of having a single code base for handling our interface needs, we could focus our development efforts on the engines underlying our products. We could better develop newer, more innovative utilities and we could focus on increasing the speed of our existing utilities to make them more competitive with other products. A fairly sizable amount of code and programming was devoted to user-interface code. This was compounded because we developed separate libraries for both of the platforms we developed for: DOS and Macintosh. With our Windows efforts just beginning, we were looking at yet another platform-specific code base to develop and maintain.

Unfortunately, two circumstances came into play at this point. One was that Bedrock had been originally designed with OS/2 as its base, and therefore the first implementation of the code was for the OS/2 platform. As Bedrock was initially being designed, OS/2 was being touted as the next platform of choice for Intel-based computers. And, at the time, there was nothing that appeared to preclude this. But, as history played itself out, this was not the case, and Windows 3.0 took the prominent position.

Object-Oriented Programming at Borland

No other company attached itself so closely to object-oriented programming as Borland had. It was a definite part of the corporate culture there, mainly because Philippe Kahn, who headed the company while we were there, was such a strong believer in the capabilities and gains to be had from object orientation. At the time we joined the company (mid-1991), there were already several projects underway that were being designed and developed in C++. All the language products the company was developing were object-oriented in nature. And the strategic core of Borland's future products orbited around each other in an object-oriented universe.

Unfortunately, due mainly to market forces, Borland was not able to reap the full benefits of its object-oriented endeavors at the time this book was written. Although these market forces were, for the most part, out of the company's control, the manner in which object orientation was used, along with certain political forces within the company, made it difficult to fully benefit from object-oriented programming.

A Period of Decline

At the time this book was written (mid-1994), there is little to show for Borland's dedication to the object-oriented discipline. Due mainly to a decrease in the profit margins of its software products, the company is in a lengthy downward spiral which requires a significant rethinking of its strategies. The company sold off its spreadsheet development division (Quattro Pro) to Novell. Many proficient C++ programmers have been laid off from the company. The object-oriented universe that was to be the core of Borland's business has virtually collapsed.

This decline in profit margins that affected the company so strongly is largely out of the company's control. A price war in high-end applications, like spreadsheets and databases (which are the core of Borland's revenue engine), is forcing the retail price of these products from several hundred dollars down into the under-$100 range. This is a significant drop in a short period of time, and it is forcing the company to examine what it is currently doing and make a rapid change in order to cut costs, focus its energies in a few key areas, and decrease the development cycle for its products.

Strangely enough, these things—cutting costs and shortening the development cycle—are two of the major goals of object-oriented programming. Why then might Borland fail when it has devoted so much to object orientation? From our perspective, which was down deep in the development trenches, it seems that although the company as a whole is devoted to object orientation, Borland's organizational structure precludes maximizing its usage.

Development Units

In a fashion similar to Symantec and a few other companies, Borland built its empire through the acquisition of other smaller companies and their products. To integrate these acquisitions into the organization, Borland took the approach of creating what were called *Development Units*. By the time we joined Borland in mid-1991, there were three primary Development Units: Languages, Databases, and Spreadsheets. Each was in effect its own company, at least from an organizational standpoint, although not from a financial standpoint. Each Unit consisted of two sections: Development and Business Affairs. The Development section focused on the actual development of the products and consisted of the software developers, quality assurance engineers, technical documentors, a manager for each section, and support staff. The Business Affairs section was in charge of handling the manufacturing and marketing of the products under the Unit's umbrella.

As can be expected, each of the three primary Development Units was focused with a specific category of product. The Languages Unit was concerned with the development of the programming languages and associated tools. Its products included Turbo Pascal, Borland C++, and Resource Workshop. The Databases Unit developed the database products: Paradox, dBASE, and ObjectVision. Finally, the Spreadsheets Unit focused on the development of the various versions of Quattro Pro, as well as other utilities such as SideKick.

The reasoning behind the creation of these Development Units was sound. They were designed to be lean and mean, a small company-within-a-company that could best handle the development and marketing of the products within the Unit. Each knew the marketplace its products competed in. Each had a handle on its customers and could best respond to their needs. These smaller organizations had a wide ranging autonomy, with little intervention from senior management within Borland. From this viewpoint, these Development Units were successful. It placed the micromanagment of product development and marketing where it needed to be: as far from the top of the hierarchy as possible.

Each of these Development Units were, however, little kingdoms, with their own agendas. The political maneuverings that were a result of these little kingdoms produced what became, in our opinion, an unhealthy division within the overall company. Territorial lines began appearing, and the flow of information between the Units was strained. The main thing missing, from a developer's standpoint, was some sort of cohesiveness between each of the Development sections of the Units. There was little difference between what a developer in any of the Units did; yet there was little cross-communication and sharing of information between programmers in different Development Units.

Wanted: Code Sharing

What was needed was more sharing of code, algorithms, and development strategies. Ironically, sharing these is one of the side-effects of utilizing the object-oriented discipline. A class library available to all the developers throughout the company could have provided a significant base for reusable code, code that was being re-implemented within each of the Units. Just like Symantec's Bedrock, an interface class library could have simplified the development of products for each of the Units and prevented waste.

Quattro Pro for Windows

With nearly three years in development, Quattro Pro for Windows was a significant project developed by the Spreadsheet Development Unit. It was one of the first Borland products to be developed in C++. With the exception of its main calculation, algorithms, the product was designed and implemented from scratch. One of its by-products was a rich class library, one that could not only be used to create a spreadsheet application, but other products as well.

Near the end of initial development of Quattro Pro for Windows—whose code name was Thor—the manager of the DOS Sidekick development team saw a potential for utilizing Thor's class library as a foundation for a whole suite of products. One of the interesting interface elements that Thor brought to the table were tabbed spreadsheet pages, as if they were contained in a notebook. Using the notebook as a metaphor, it was realized that a future Sidekick-like product could be developed, where each of the "pages" of the notebook was an application. In a rather short period of time, a small prototype was developed and presented to management, who quickly bought off on the idea and a development team was put together.

While Thor was being polished up for final shipment, we split off a version of the class library's code base and began making modifications to better enable it as a basis for our application. In retrospect, it would have been advantageous had each of the Development Units been aware of, and perhaps had a hand in, the modifications we were making. From an organizational standpoint, it would have been good if we all had gathered together to design a class library which would have met all of our needs.

A Cross Platform Class Library

Looking back on it now, it seems a significant opportunity was missed by not doing this. At the time, however, we were concerned, just as all the other Units were, about what was best for our own project. It wasn't until later in its development that senior management saw this class library could be utilized as a base for applications throughout the company. A team dedicated to the creation and maintenance of a cross-platform class library was brought together under the auspices of the Spreadsheet Development Unit.

Trying to get the other Development Units to buy-off on this new class library was an impossible task. The main weakness of this class library was that it had not been fully designed as a base from which differing types of applications could be built. As expected, it was originally designed as the basis of spreadsheet applications. Later, design and implementation modifications were made so that it could better be used first as the basis of another unrelated product, then as a cross-platform development tool. However, it was still a fairly rigid and monolithic library that was difficult for the other Development Units to adopt. This was primarily because it would require a virtual rewrite of their existing code. As is typical in commercial software development, there was little or no time for this activity, no matter how much could potentially be gained at a later time.

The Development Units were primarily concerned with their own agendas, which consisted of maintaining the status quo. The flagship product in each of the Units had a large code-base with a rich history. In order to fully utilize a cross-organization, the class library would have required a substantial redevelopment of the existing code base. None of the Units had either the resources or the time available to accomplish this.

With the number and quality of developers Borland had, it is too bad more could not have been done on this front. But due to the organizational composition of the company, Borland was not able to fully utilize its object-oriented resources. Outside market forces further prevented the company from instituting an organization-wide, object-oriented development strategy and class library by the time we left the company in mid-1993.

Conclusion

In retrospect, none of the experiences we've just recounted for you have lived up to their full potential, due mainly to unfortunate circumstances. From a developer's standpoint, there are obvious benefits to be had from object-oriented methodologies. Code reuse, simplified extensibility, enhanced maintenance of the code, and easier portability of code to other platforms all help shorten the development time and therefore lower the cost of the development.

Unfortunately, in the real world of commercial software development, there are often other overriding considerations that prevent us from fully utilizing what object-oriented development has to offer. Perhaps the single most difficult obstacle to overcome is that the benefits are of a long-term nature, whereas the business of software manufacturing is, like many businesses, primarily concerned with short-term results.

Our efforts at Peter Norton Computing were, unfortunately, at an early stage for the company and in the history of object-oriented software development. This precluded us—from a business standpoint—from undertaking the object-oriented development effort. Both Symantec and Borland attempted to take a long-term approach to their development efforts. Circumstances within the two companies—primarily of a managerial, organizational, and financial nature—prevented either company from fully benefiting from their object-oriented development efforts.

In the case of Borland, its organizational composition and the stresses on its finances proved to be too difficult a burden when it came to its long-term efforts. The pains from the acquisition of Ashton-Tate, along with the drop in profit-margins within the industry as software prices fell, meant the company had to reorganize and refocus its efforts on mere survival. It is nearly impossible for the management of a company to accommodate any potential benefits to be had at a later time when the question of whether the company is even going to be around in the future is raised. It seems that the best use for the object-oriented discipline is for products that are being built from the ground up. It has been difficult for companies in the commercial software industry to take the time and resources to redesign and re-implement an existing base of code. In order to fully utilize the benefits of object orientation much thought and planning must go into the design and subsequent implementation of a class library.

A company that may turn out to have successfully integrated object-oriented programming into the commercial software development environment is Microsoft. Although the competitive pressures are the same for them as any other company in the industry, the impact of a dwindling profit-margin is minimized. As both an operating system and application developer, Microsoft is able to absorb more of a loss to its profit-margin than many other companies, Borland and Symantec included.

Licensing of its Disk Operating System for IBM-PC compatibles has provided an incredible infusion of cash into Microsoft for over a decade now. With not just a buffer, but a steady flow of cash into the company, Microsoft is better situated to take more time to carefully design and develop its applications programs.

This was clearly enunciated to us at a developer's conference a few years back with the unveiling of Microsoft's Visual C++. At one point during the announcement, a representative of the company stated that its original class library that was developed for the product was a failure—its code size was extremely large and the objects in the library were cumbersome to use.

So a significant—both in time and resultant cost—redesign and subsequent reimplementation replaced the original class library. This new class library—The Microsoft Foundation Library (MFC)—is, in many programmers' opinions, one of the main selling points for Visual C++.

In this chapter we've seen that object-oriented languages encompass the following things:

- Object-oriented languages enable the programmer to construct classes that are abstract data types. These classes provide for both *encapsulation*—the binding of the data type and its associated group of functions that operate on the data into a single object and *data hiding*—whereby access to the members of the class by other classes is limited.

- Through the concept of *inheritance*, new classes can be created that are derived from other existing classes.

- Virtual functions enable the programmer to specify different actions for classes derived from a base class.

We've also seen that some of the benefits to be gained from OOP are:

- Reusability of both data and code

- Enhanced ability to maintain existing code

- Cross-platform development

We concluded by taking a look at how object-oriented programming has been used at some of the companies we've worked at.

Chapter 5

Debugging

One of the great truths in life is that humans are flawed creatures. A side-effect of this is that their creations are flawed as well. Unfortunately, this includes the software we write.

Currently, there seem to be many schools of thought as to what to call a "problem" with a piece of software. "Bug" is the term given to us by programming pioneer Grace Hopper (after finding a moth in one of the first computers). Others prefer a more harsh term such as "flaw" or "defect." They argue that "bug" is too cute, it is too easily ignored as being just a minor problem. They say that by using "flaw" or "defect," they are conveying the severity of the problem.

Personally, we still prefer "bug." It's short, it doesn't sting, and it still conveys the meaning. We don't see any point in using words that are harsh or inflammatory. To paraphrase The Bard: "A bug is a bug is a bug. A bug by any other name would still stink."

The Politics of Bugs (or Protecting Your Sanity)

Before we get into how to find and fix bugs, we're going to talk about our experiences with the ramifications of bugs. Everyone seems to have a different viewpoint on bugs, and everyone wants to have their finger in the pie. Anyone who doesn't want their finger in that proverbial pie, wants to throw it at you.

Many people have a hard time accepting that bugs are a fact of life. They point at bridges and roads. They say if we can build those big things without problems, why is it so hard to add a simple feature without breaking something? After all, this is software engineering, right? Wrong. This is software development. These people probably won't ever understand that writing software is not a science and that "a simple, little feature" never is. Just grin and get out your Nerf bat. This is an action everyone understands.

As a software developer, there is a certain unwritten job you have. It's your responsibility to be the advocate for clean, bug-free code. Nobody else is in a good position to do this. Management wants it done. Marketing wants something to sell. Technical Support and your customers just want it to work. Your goals and theirs can only be met through clean code. It's likely to have fewer bugs. It's easier to add new features to clean code. Other developers doing maintenance on it can read and understand it easier.

Make clean code your personal mantra. Repeat it many times every day. Seriously, the only thing better than maintaining clean code is writing it. There is a certain satisfaction that comes with writing clean code. It's really nice to look back at the code you've just written and see that it's well put together, it's easy to read, and that it should be fairly straightforward to maintain. Besides, a couple years from now you want to be able to look at the code you wrote today and say "I did a good job," rather than "I wrote *that*?!?"

Management and Marketing

In the political bug area, these folks can be the most irritating. This is probably because they are putting pressure on you to meet the schedule they set and pressured you to agree to. Now that you've agreed to the schedule, they expect you to keep it (regardless of the number of feature additions, design changes, and priority shifts that happen along the way).

Don't get me wrong; these guys are doing the right thing—from their point of view. Remember, your goal as a developer is to do a good job, which means clean, working code. Nobody else truly cares if it's clean, just if it works. After all, the end user doesn't see the source code; they only get the executable. To everyone besides yourself, this is all that really counts.

The best thing to do with these people is to sit down and find out what bugs they consider important. Make a list of these bugs. Make sure they sign off on this list (this ensures everyone is aware of the situation).

They will likely ask you for an estimated date of completion at this meeting. Don't give them one. You will be very tempted to give one. After all, this *is* your boss. But, this would be an off-the-cuff estimate of the completion date. You're very likely to be wrong. Simply tell them you need to go back and do a little research. Schedule another meeting with them so you can present them with your plan of attack and estimated date of completion.

Go back to your office or cubicle and make a list of the bugs you think are important. As the developer, you should know what bugs are really serious. Make sure they're on the list.

Combine the two lists—the list you got from your boss and the list of bugs you know to be important. Now you are ready to make an estimate. Be reasonable. Don't over-estimate your ability to fix some bugs. If there are some unknowns, be honest. It is better to say that you're not sure up-front, than to have to get a schedule changed later on.

You should also prepare an estimate for only the bugs that your boss feels are important. This is something he or she definitely wants to know. With both of these estimates, your boss can see the cost *and* benefits of the bugs you added to the "to do" list. Bosses like that a lot.

When you go to the scheduled meeting, bring both of your lists and their estimates. Explain what bugs you added to create your list and why. Put it in straightforward terms like "data might be lost," or "it could crash in the worst case." Be honest about it. Developers, managers, and marketers don't all speak the same language. In fact, sometimes you have to wonder if we're really all human. But there are some areas where we all agree and some phrases we all understand. "Crash" and "lost" are definitely in everyone's vocabulary, especially when they're used in the same sentence as "data." Many years ago we worked on a project where we had a nasty bug that would periodically overwrite a random field of a data record while saving it to disk. This bug wasn't given very high priority (we were a small company with few programming resources). They finally gave me the time to fix it after we pointed out that this could easily be a wild pointer that could be doing other things when not clobbering a field.

If you go to them prepared with all the information they need to decide, they'll usually do what you recommend (in this case, at least; this doesn't always hold true for raises). By being prepared and educating them, you have accomplished three things. First, and most important, you will have furthered your goal of clean code. Second, you are helping educate your manager. Next time you have to deal with bugs, you may find they are more likely to implement your plan of attack. Lastly, if this is done right, you have shown your manager that you are thorough. This *does* help with raises.

Customers and Technical Support

These folks are two sides of the same coin. In fact, a good technical support department is really a "customer advocate" department. These folks just want one thing: a working product. The only trouble with them is that everything is urgent. Sometimes they expect you to drop everything and help fix this problem. They're only repeating what the client is saying to them.

At first, this is really annoying. But, it can definitely be used in your favor. You are the software developer. Your job is to be chained to your computer, producing code. A technical support person's job is to deal with the customer. It's not hard to get them to help you with the bug-fixing process. You just have to ask.

When they come to you with a problem, get as much information as you can. If they cannot supply you with enough data, ask them for more. Quite often a technical support person goes back to the client and asks more questions if you ask them to. Give them specific questions to ask and procedures to do. This makes their job easier and you significantly increase your chances of getting good information.

You should remember that customers are the people who have paid for your software and are the people using it. Quite often a good customer knows how to do things you never dreamed of. Make these people your friends. They have a view of the product that, as a developer, is difficult to get.

Technical support people can be great allies, or they can be real nuisances. How it ends up is in your hands. Sometimes it's worth buying the technical support department a box of doughnuts, a bag of bagels, or whatever snack they like. The small amount of money is worth the help you'll get.

You *do* have to watch out for these guys. Sometimes marketing and technical support will team up and try to slip a new feature request in as a bug report. This is a bad plan. Don't let them get away with it. New features should go through a review and design process before being slipped into the system.

Sometimes it's easier to avoid the issue altogether. Getting your bugs out of an on-line bug list is definitely less stressful than having someone standing over your shoulder waiting for you to fix the bug he just found. One sneaky way to avoid contact with technical support is to avoid being known for being on a particular project. Once they know you're on a project, they'll be tempted to call you when they have a problem with that project.

One time I was busy in my office, coding my heart out. My phone rings and I presume it's my girlfriend calling to let me know she was in the lobby (we were going out to lunch that day). Naturally, it wasn't. It was a technical support person. He had a customer on the line with a problem with the previous project I worked on. In fact, the customer wasn't just on the line, they were both on the line with me (conference call). Needless to say I was late for lunch (fortunately, my girlfriend was understanding). And, the technical support guy and his boss got quite an earful from me. The moral of this story is: Try to be invisible to technical support personnel.

Quality Assurance

In my experience, there are two types of QA departments: the ones you like and the ones you don't. Both of them are hunting down any bugs in the code. Both of them manage beta tests. Both of them make fun of the bugs they find. And, both of them seriously test the limits of your sanity (if you have any left).

Their differences lie in how they deal with the bugs they find. A good QA department will be light-hearted about the ribbing you get for a bug in your code. They laugh with you and ask how you could possibly let that bug by. After that, they sit down and help you find and kill the bug they found. They do further testing if you need it. They make sample databases for you should a bug require it. In other words, these guys are your friends. They're part of the team.

On the other hand, a bad QA department establishes an adversarial relationship with you. They take great pleasure in finding bugs in your code. They laugh at you, sneer at you, and even circulate rumors that question your lineage. Well, maybe they won't go that far. But, you find you're questioning theirs.

A bad QA department makes the whole debugging, beta test, and bug resolution/extermination process a real chore. Typically, once they find a bug and report it they consider their job to be done. If you can't recreate it, too bad, you're not getting their help. After all, you wrote the code that had the bug, it's your problem. You're lucky they even bothered to tell you about it.

Some schools of project management seem to think this style of adversarial relationship encourages the software developers to produce bug-free code. They think the developers will work harder to find and fix their own bugs before releasing the code to QA. Quite often the results are worse than if the bugs go unfixed. The developer's goal is to get QA off of his back as soon as possible. Rather than fixing a bug properly, code ends up being fixed with smoke, mirrors, duct tape, and chewing gum. This might work on TV, but it doesn't work in software development.

Fortunately, as the software development environment matures, good QA departments are springing up everywhere. People are finding that better code is produced in an environment where QA and developers cooperate. A humorous, mildly competitive, but definitely cooperative relationship works very, very well. A good QA department is great to work with. After all, do you want to go test every single feature of your product every time you make a release? Do you want to start, manage, and report on the beta tests your product goes through? We didn't think so.

Your Peers

These people run the entire length of the spectrum. Each development department is different. In a good department, most people lean heavily toward being helpful.

In one place where I worked, I started the "Bug of the Week." Whenever I would do something really stupid that I spent hours trying to track down, I would announce it to my teammates. This caught on for quite a while. It led to a relaxed and productive environment. Various bugs of the week included:

- Never divide by zero.

- Always check the printer's power switch before you presume the report printing engine is broken.

- Initialize your variables before you use them, especially when they're pointers.

- Always open a file before reading from it.

- If you want to test the changes you made in the code, compile it before you try running it.

- Always log on to the network before you attempt to try out the network communications module.

- Never free up dynamically allocated memory before you're done with it. Better yet: Never free up memory before you allocate it.

Needless to say, we all had a few laughs at my expense. Everyone can see and admit that they did stupid things, too. When it came time to tackle real bugs, nobody was afraid to bring them up. We all knew that bugs were an unfortunate part of the process.

Progress

Like the rest of the development process, it's important to maintain some momentum. If you are fixing bug after bug, you are likely to make good progress. On the other hand, if you get bogged down with one bug, you are likely to lose some of your momentum. This can result in a drastic decrease in your productivity.

Keeping things going is good for everyone. Nobody likes to see a project at a stand-still (least of all, your boss). Lack of progress, if it goes on too long, can actually affect morale. Low morale can kill a project. One project we worked on a few years ago was devastated by the first-line manager. The team was excited about the project; we were ready to go. In meeting after meeting this manager shot down our designs, telling us that they weren't what he wanted. But, he wouldn't tell us *what* he wanted. So, week after week we came back to him with new plans. Each time he would shoot them down. Finally, after a month of this, we didn't care about the project. A team of developers that started out really excited about this project ended up not even caring if it even got done. Avoid low morale; it's not good for a project.

When we get hit with a bug that really bogs me down, we move on to a few small bugs. Fixing two, three, or even a dozen of these small bugs tends to restore my momentum. While we're fixing these small bugs, we also find that we come up with possible solutions to the big problem we're facing. We guess this is parallel processing of a sort.

Your Time

Now, let's be honest. Do you really want to spend your time debugging your code? Of course not. Nobody does. We got into software to build things. Debugging gets in the way. If we could get away without doing it, we would.

Some of you may be shocked to read that. We're only writing what most people are thinking. Bugs aren't fun. The fact that they exist in your code is a blatant reminder that you aren't perfect. Debugging isn't glorious. It's drudge work that we all wish could be passed off on someone else.

Sometimes your wish comes true. You're working on a vital part of a project and a bug is reported in another part of your code. You don't have time to fix the bug and get this needed feature done, too. So, someone else gets volunteered to fix the bug. Enjoy it when this happens.

Unfortunately, sometimes someone else gets to pass it off to you. Debugging someone else's code is like straightening out their bedroom. You get to see all of the interesting things they have, but you also have to deal with the mess. The fun you have seeing their foibles wears off very quickly. It quickly turns into just another debugging session.

One way to look at this that makes it a little easier: you don't have much of a choice. You just have to do it. Buggy software usually doesn't sell well. It certainly doesn't get good reviews. So, you could easily be missing out on the fame, fortune, glory, and money by not getting rid of a few bugs.

Another pattern we have noticed: People who write clean code don't end up doing much maintenance work. This doesn't mean they don't debug their code. This just means they aren't the ones modifying and updating the utilities. They aren't the ones writing batch files and installation programs. They are the glory hounds building bigger and better software.

Given all this, I still think debugging is no fun. I simply tell myself that I don't get to build more until I fix what I've already built. Plus, there is a quiet satisfaction knowing that you have clean, "bug-free" code. (We use quotes there, because no significant piece of code is free of bugs; they just haven't been discovered yet.)

Extermination

One of the basic tenets of journalism is to get the facts. There's a simple list that covers this pretty well: who, what, when, why, where, and how? Who is the article about? What happened? When did it happen? Why did it happen? Where did it happen? And, how did it happen?

This holds true for debugging, too. It's important to get a good feel for bugs that exist. Do not treat all the bugs as individual problems to be fixed. Quite often many of the bugs are related in some way. Fixing the root cause can get rid of all the related bugs. Getting to check off five or six bugs at a time is really fun.

Fixing bugs is not a very well defined process. It can be done in nearly any way as long as the clean code results. You should really read over the bug list first. And, you *must* reproduce the bug prior to fixing it. After all, if you can't make it happen, how do you know if you fixed it? The answer is, you don't. Even if someone shows you a bug, reproduce it for yourself.

Aside from these two steps, the rest of the process is somewhat freeform. Do what you find comfortable. Use the tools that make you the most productive. As with the rest of the software development process, being comfortable with the debugging process you use is very important.

The Bug Pool (Who)

Knowing your players is very important. Each bug gives you a clue into the workings of the system. Taken as a whole, the list of bugs in a system can be very enlightening. Related bugs can be strewn about the complete bug list. Multi-symptom bugs can be listed in many different places (for example, when you have the flu, you have a stuffy nose *and* a cough).

Prior to sitting down to tackle some bugs, read the entire list of known bugs. Sometimes this sparks a few good ideas that make the process easier. Sometimes you can determine the solution for a bug without looking at the code. Finding even a few bugs this way can save you a lot of time.

Bugs that are on your list of bugs "to do" are quite often related to those that are not. Examining these related bugs gives you a perspective on a bug you might have missed. As we pointed out above, this can be invaluable.

Being well versed in the complete bug list can also help when your teammates ask for help. Hopefully, they will have read the list when you ask them for help.

Replicating the Bug (What)

This can be one of the toughest parts of debugging. It would be nice if we lived in a perfect world where bug reports stated exactly how to duplicate a particular problem.

But, we don't, so sometimes we must track down a bug that may be described like "program crashes when the user enters data." What data? In what part of the program? Sometimes users don't know that you need more data. Sometimes the user doesn't have the data you need.

Since we usually get bug reports from people in the QA department (see Chapter 6, "Quality Assurance"), we can go down the hall and ask them questions. Usually this trip results in a lucid answer. Sometimes it'll be something on the order of "Well, I'm not sure. I was banging on the table management screen and it just bombed out to the OS."

Even though this is vague, be thankful it is polite. Bug reports that come from marketing and technical support departments are not always polite (or lucid). When these types of bug reports come in, remember, you work for the same company (even if it seems like they've forgotten). They probably have a customer calling them every hour asking about the bug in question.

In any case, not all bug reports are complete. It's your job to make every attempt to figure out how to cause this bug. Sometimes this isn't possible. Show the bug report to a teammate or friend. Sometimes a second set of eyes can really help.

If you have made a good attempt at replicating this bug and still cannot make it happen, go over the source code by hand. Step through it in your head. Speak each step out loud. People may look at you as if you are nuts, but you would be surprised what you can find this way.

Sometimes a bug only occurs on certain hardware. This is pretty rare, but still happens. Tracking this kind of bug down is difficult. If you can, try to reproduce an elusive bug on the machine where it first happened. If that's not possible, try to find or build a computer with a similar configuration.

If you still cannot reproduce it, kick it back to the source. Try to get more information. A bug you cannot reproduce is one you cannot fix. Why spend time trying to recreate a bug when there may be others you could quickly fix?

What Happened Before the Problem? (When)

Most of the time a bug occurs regardless of what is done prior to hitting a particular section of the code. Sometimes, though, a bug requires that two or more things happen in a particular order.

With bugs like these, it's important to know what the user did and in what order. This is another good reason to encourage complete bug reports. You need the complete order of operations to replicate a bug like this.

Once you can reproduce this bug, look at what happens in the initial steps of the bug report. Quite often, these sections of code are setting up a situation that causes the final step(s) to fail.

Once you see what's going on, ask yourself: Is the problem in the initial sections where the data is getting set or generated incorrectly? Or, is the problem in the final sections where the data is being used wrong?

Finding the Source of the Problem (Where)

You can't find a bug without knowing where it is. Finding the specific place where a bug occurs can be tough. It may not be obvious or simple.

There are a number of ways to track a bug down. We've listed a few here. There are other ways, but we feel that most are a combination of the methods below. Undoubtedly, there are other general methods in use out in the field. But, we are not aware of them. Nobody knows everything.

When you're tracking down a bug, use the method that makes the most sense. Once again, you should be comfortable with what you're doing. This doesn't mean you shouldn't learn new things. It just means you shouldn't be forcing your way through things. It's less productive.

Debuggers

Debuggers are your best friend. Modern compilers (such as Microsoft Visual C++ and Borland C++) come with nice integrated debuggers.

Learn to use your debugger well. In the long run, nothing will help you kill bugs more than your debugger. You can find just about all bugs using just your debugger. Sometimes, however, you don't want to. It's not the most sophisticated of tools.

It is well suited for finding minor flaws. If a particular function is returning a bad value or if a piece of code is executing when it shouldn't, you can use your debugger to find out the state of the program at these points. A good debugger, such as the ones that come with the Microsoft and Borland C++ products, let you step through your source code watching variables as they change. This can be *very* informative.

Use this to help wrap up bugs you have located with other techniques. This is where your debugger functions best. After you track down a nasty bug using some other technique, you can use your debugger to confirm all your findings.

Status Messages

Some bugs are hard to track down using just the debugger. This technique helps you track down problems with bad data, the wrong piece of code being executed, and so on.

This is also an excellent technique to use on machines where you don't have a debugger. Machines at an end-user site probably won't have a debugger on them. In fact, you'll be lucky if you run the program yourself. In cases like this, using a Log File (see the next section) might be a better option.

This is simply printing a message to a screen. How you print it to the screen can vary depending on your environment. In a UNIX, DOS, or other character-mode environment, you can simply print the message. Under X/Windows, Windows, or on a Mac, you can pop up a little message box.

The message can include just about anything. Make sure that it's meaningful to you. You can put as many of these messages in the code as you need.

Log Files

Sometimes your program has a bug that occurs in the middle of a lot of processing. Maybe a few records get garbled when scanning a database, or some lines disappear in a text file processor. Whatever the case, log files are great when you have a bug that happens infrequently when processing a lot of stuff.

This is a more intense variation of the Status Messages technique. This method allows you to see what's going on in non-real time. Like the Status Messages technique, this is also an excellent method to use on a machine where you don't have a debugger. It's really nice on end-user machines. They can run the program, get the bug to occur, and then send you the log file. This way, you don't have to deal with a technical support person's interpretation of what the end-user *thinks* the program is doing.

Make sure you have enough information in the log file to track down the bug. It is far better to put lots of information in the log file. Too little information means that you have to run the program again. If it's just you, all you lose is a little time. This is bad enough. But, if you ask an end-user to run the program over and over, they're going to be a little less understanding. Most of them do not understand the bug hunting process—nor do they care to know. They just want the software to work.

Once you figure out where the problem is, you can examine the code that causes the problem. With a good log file, you should be able to determine the location of the bug down to within a couple lines of code.

At this point, you know which piece of data made the program bomb. Feed this to the program and see if the bug occurs again. If so, you know you have a small data set that makes the bug happen. No more waiting for the big data set to run.

Now that you have this small data set in hand, get out your debugger and feed the data set to the program. Step through it with your debugger. You should see the bug in action. Gruesome!

Process of Elimination

This technique is good for bugs that freeze or crash out to the operating system. It isn't very useful for most other bugs.

Sometimes a bug keeps itself well hidden to standard techniques. It knows you're looking for it and takes precautions. That's probably a little paranoid. But, sometimes it seems that way. Bugs can be very elusive.

Selectively commenting out code can tell you a lot. In the area where you figure the bug lives, comment out practically everything. Run the program to make sure it doesn't crash or bomb-out anymore. If it still does, expand the part you comment out until it stops crashing.

Now that you can run the program without crashing, make the area you've commented out smaller. Don't make it much smaller. The goal here is to figure out which piece of code contains the bug. Big jumps make that harder. Continue to run and uncomment until you get the bug again.

Now that you get the bug again, you know the cause of the bug is in the area you just uncommented. If you made the area small enough, you can find the bug pretty easily.

Now you need to comment out the block with the bug and uncomment everything else. Then, run the program again. This, in effect, double checks that the bug is in that section. If the program doesn't crash, you *know* the bug is in that small snippet of code. If it still does, start commenting out other sections of code. Keep doing this until you have a program that runs without crashing—with a minimal amount of code commented out.

You now can examine the small section of code more closely. If you choose, you can use this technique to narrow the problem down to the specific line.

Identifying the Cause (Why)

Bugs don't just "happen." They are put there by you and your teammates. You don't mean to do it. Nobody does, we hope. But, the fact of the matter is, when you were creating the software, you created it with bugs. Oops.

There are many styles of bugs. There are bugs that overwrite random memory, bugs that put the processor into an infinite loop, bugs that crash the program entirely, bugs that delete data, and bugs that trash your hard disk. If it's bad, we're sure a bug has done it. Bugs are kind of like the Infinite Number of Monkeys—if you get enough of them, they're bound to do something you really don't want.

Many kinds of bugs leave "fingerprints." Certain kinds of bugs behave in more specific ways. Granted, "more specific" is relative, since any given bug can do just about anything. Individual bugs (except wild pointers) tend to act in a specific fashion. But, taken as a whole, bugs are a pretty random lot.

Use these clues to determine what method to use when tracking the bug. Knowing what kind of bug it might be can really help in the debugging process. It helps you look for specific kinds of problems in the code. But, don't spend too much time looking for specific things. Your assumption about the style of bug can easily be wrong. It's really annoying to spend a couple hours looking in the wrong place.

Obviously, all of the types of bugs cannot be listed here. As we pointed out above, there's a bug for every occasion. Listed below are the bugs we encounter most often. These are the ones you should be most familiar with.

Bad Logic

This is absolutely the most common cause of bugs. Fortunately, it's the simplest to fix. Unfortunately, it's the easiest to miss. The brain is amazingly good at reading what it wants to read. When examining a piece of your own code, your brain sometimes sees what it wants to, rather than what it should.

When examining your own code, treat it as if it were someone else's. Examine every piece very closely. Look for small errors (they have a tendency to snowball into big ones). Look for a misplaced semi-colon, or a greater-than where you should've had a less-than. Look for loops that go in the wrong direction (going up, where they should have gone down).

Sometimes handing a listing to one of your teammates is the easiest way to handle one of these. Tell them what the code is supposed to do. Since they haven't dealt with that part of the code repeatedly as you have, they might spot the bug very quickly.

On one of the better development teams I've been on over the years, the guy I shared my office with would always come to me with bugs like these. I would hear him pulling his hair out for about half an hour. Then, he would pop his head over the cubicle wall and ask me to look at a certain piece of code. Quite often I would find it within about a minute of pulling it up. Sometimes *much* faster. Usually it was something really small like a misplaced end-of-statement marker.

Bad Input (GIGO)

Most software requires some kind of input from the user. And, as we all know, users will enter just about anything. It's our job to make sure a little bad data from the user doesn't crash the system.

This kind of problem is very easily averted. Whenever you write a section of code that handles user input, ensure the data is clean before it enters the rest of the system. If you do this, other parts of the software don't have to be as vigilant when using data entered by the user. In some instances, this can greatly reduce code complexity.

These bugs are fairly easy to spot. Typical bug reports read "user typed his name into the zip code field and the system puked."

Bad input can come from other places, too. Corrupted data files or line noise on a serial line are two classic examples. Corruption can occur wherever data enters the software. This can easily be avoided by checking all data that enters the system. Again, once the data is in and verified you don't have to worry about it.

Bugs like these are fairly straightforward to spot as well. The bug reports usually refer to some kind of input into the program, followed by the program reporting bad data, spewing garbage, locking, or just crashing. A typical report might read "user copied data file from old version and the program spewed garbage" or "we got some line noise on the modem and the program locked up."

Buffer Overruns

This kind of bug is caused by putting, copying, and so forth, a piece of data into a buffer that is too small. A buffer overrun can be pretty obvious. It usually results in either corrupted data, valid data in the wrong place, or a crash. A crash sometimes occurs because the information the computer needs to exit the function gets overwritten.

Sometimes you won't find one of these until months into a project. Since these bugs are pretty easy to fix, it's not a big deal. But, even this can be avoided by decent testing on your part. Wherever you have a data entry field, fill it. This catches 99 percent of these bugs.

A good QA department will find it very quickly. They test for the extremes that cause bugs like these. Remember, don't rely on them to do all your testing. They're more of a safety net.

The bug reports for buffer overruns are pretty obvious. You'll get reports like "if you type in a long filename, the last half of the filename ends up the user name field" or "after typing in a long address, the program crashes."

Data or Structure Size Differences

These bugs can be sneaky. You change a variable from single-precision floating point to double-precision. Or, you add a member to a structure or class. This is pretty common during the initial process of building a project or a new feature.

The next thing you know, part of the code causes really bizarre things to happen. Data that went into it correct comes out garbled. Often the first element of an array of structures seems fine, but subsequent elements seem garbled. Data items that have changed in size end up with strange data. Classes that have changed end up with data being placed in the wrong elements.

What we have here is a failure to recompile. This usually happens when one of your modules didn't get compiled with the updated definitition for your variable, class, or structure. This means that the majority of your program is using the new definition, while this errant module is still using the old. With classes and structures, this can easily mean that the module using the old definition is getting and placing data in entirely the wrong locations.

Whenever you change the size or type of a variable or whenever you change a class or structure, recompile everything. This can take a little extra time, but you avoid any problems that may arise. In fact, if you have your compiler set to its maximum warning level, it should tell you about any incompatibilities that came of the change (such as precision loss with floating point data, data conversion problems, and so on).

Uninitialized Variables

Another classic bug. You declare all of your variables. You initialize most of them to their desired values. But, you forget one. Everything seems fine, though. Your code compiles without complaint. And, it seems to go along just fine. You're feeling good about the new code you added. Time to move on to the next new feature.

Then, suddenly, you get this really odd value out of one of your computational routines, or, the code pauses for a couple of seconds for some strange reason. These and any number of other things can be the result of an uninitialized variable.

This type of bug has no real characterization. It can manifest itself in many different ways. What happens, and when, is highly dependent upon the code and the value (usually random) of the uninitialized variable. Stepping through the errant code with a good debugger is the best way to track down a bug like this. Be sure to watch most (or all) of the important variables within the module. You should be able to spot the value that is wrong merely by inspection at this point. If not, watch the values carefully and see which one of them causes the code to misbehave.

This bug may become a thing of the past. Modern compilers can warn you about this. This is one of the many good reasons to turn the warning level on your compiler as high as it will go. This helps you catch potential problems long before they happen. Catching these problems early saves you from having to deal with them later when you're looking down the barrel of an impending deadline.

Wild Pointers

No, this is not a club for hunting dogs that like to party.

Wild pointers are pointers that are not pointing where they should. Quite often, these are pointed at some random location in memory. Consequently, this can be a tough type of bug to find. Most of the time, this type of bug is caused by an uninitialized pointer (see the previous section for more on this type of bug).

As we have implied, there are two basic types of these bugs. The first is where a specific location in memory is being overwritten. This is easier to track down. Modern debuggers can be told to pause execution (break) when a certain location in memory has changed. In fact, they can be told to break when that location changes to or from a specific value.

This bug reveals itself through its regularity. It writes some strange value to the same spot over and over. This can result in odd file sizes (much too small or way too big) or strange calculations. This can easily result in the program freezing up at a certain point every time (this is either the result of strange data making the program loop forever or the result of the code itself getting hit).

The second kind is a truly wild pointer. This causes random bits of memory to be overwritten. This is much harder to track down as you never know where it'll strike next. Sometimes it hits data, sometimes it hits code, sometimes it hits memory nobody is using, and sometimes it hits the operating system.

There is hope for this kind of bug. For the DOS and Windows environments there is a program called Soft-ICE. This program, with its companion Bounds Checker, waits quietly for your program to do something that it shouldn't (for example, write to a part of memory it shouldn't, use a port that it shouldn't, and so on).

This can be tricky and tedious to track down. Sometimes you have to do a lot of fiddling with the packages. It's worth it. If you think you have a wild pointer, start looking. Due to their random nature, these bugs have the potential to do massive damage. Nothing can make a program look worse than many various random bugs that result in data corruption or loss. One wild pointer can make your entire product look poorly written.

As stated above, this is one of the hardest bugs to diagnose. Your only real clue to this is seemingly random bugs happening all around the system. If one of these bugs occurs frequently, you may be able to track down the wild pointer by waiting for its symptom to occur.

Fixing the Problem (How)

Once you've tracked the problem down to its source, you should be able to get rid of the bug. You've suffered the pain of tracking the bug down; now it's time to kill it.

You know what the code is supposed to do, so just change it to make it do that. This is usually pretty straight-forward. Most bugs are created by small, easily-fixed (once identified) errors. Sometimes being small and easily-fixed lets a bug hide.

Sometimes the fix is not so small. You're faced with a serious flaw in your logic. In these cases, this can be a big task. Fixing this kind of bug involves fundamentally changing the way a piece of code works. You've put a lot of work into the code, so you're naturally hesitant to make this kind of change.

It can be a hassle, but, break down, make the big change. It is far better to have clean, clear code. If this means you have to do a little extra work to change the way you do things, so be it. At least this way you don't end up with something that is difficult to understand and cobbled together.

Last step, double check everything. If you introduce another bug by fixing this one, you'll have to go through this process all over again. Spend a little time testing now so you can avoid spending a lot of time debugging later.

Claiming Completion

Now you're at the end. The bug is fixed. Time to change the status of a bug to "fixed." You're feeling great. A sense of relief washes over you as you watch your code behave properly. You can hardly wait to get to the next bug and kill it, too.

Before you move on, wait. At times, a new bug is introduced when an old one is fixed. Even the most careful people get bitten here. Make sure you've really killed the bug. Make sure all the related bugs are killed, too. Double check that obscure parts of the code you just changed still work. Sometimes a minor change in one spot seriously affects things further down the line. Make sure features that rely on the code you just changed haven't broken.

Time is good reason not to prematurely claim that a bug is complete. Take a little time to test your code thoroughly before counting the bug as dead. The small amount of time you spend testing your code is nothing compared to the amount of time wasted if a bug gets into a shipping product. People have postulated that a bug which might take one hour to fix in the initial coding stages may take as much as ten or more to fix once a project has been released. This doesn't even include the costs of updating existing users, possibly modifying manuals, notifying dealers, and so on.

Remember, nothing is more embarrassing that to get bitten by the same bug over and over, especially after claiming that it has been fixed. This can really harm your reputation.

In Summary

There is no substitute for producing clean code. It is easier to maintain, it is easier to add-on to, and most importantly, it is less likely to have bugs. This, in the long run, saves you a lot of time. More time means you can write more code; which leads to more fame, money, and glory. All of this ultimately leads us back to where we started: more time to write better and more interesting code.

If you remember anything from this chapter, you should remember these points:

- Bugs are a fact of life. Live with it. Kill all the ones you know about.

- Bug-free code exists in fairy tales. Don't believe the stuff a lot of magazine columnists write. In a lot of cases, they've never dealt with real software development.

- Clean code avoids many, many problems. It's as close to bug-free code as you will get.

- Always keep your compiler set to the highest warning level. Writing warning-free code will help you produce clean code.

- The rest of the company isn't your enemy. They're just on your back to fix the code. Fix it quick and do it right.

- Learn how to use your debugger. Take a peek at some of the more obscure features. They can sometimes be of great help. This is a matter of "When you need it, you really, *really* need it."

- Keep your sense of humor alive; you'll need it. Keep your stress level down. And, if you don't have one already, go get yourself a Nerf bat.

Chapter 6

Quality Assurance

In this chapter we'll take a look at the quality assurance aspects of developing software:

- The process begins with a thorough testing of the program by the members of the Quality Assurance team.

- An Alpha Test, or testing of the program by people within the company, is the next step in the quality assurance process.

- Once the internal testing is complete, the program is released to carefully selected people outside the company in what is called the Beta Test.

- During the Beta testing period all reported bugs are carefully logged and tracked. When the number and type of bugs are at an acceptable level, the program is released for manufacturing and shipment.

One of the rather unfortunate aspects of programming is that, no matter how careful we are as developers, bugs are bound to be buried somewhere in the code we write. The bugs might not even be in code we've developed, but in how our code interacts with other code. In either case, the end result is an "anomaly," an "unexpected application error," or a "fault." It could be a situation where at best the user is chuckling because a word is misspelled, or at worst the user is screaming at the technical support person on the other end of the telephone line because a bug in the program trashed the data file, wiping out a month's worth of work. As developers, we aim to avoid bugs wherever we can. But knowing bugs are lurking somewhere in the code, we turn to Quality Assurance personnel to find those bugs—as many of them as they can—so we can fix them before the product goes out the door and into the hands of the end users.

Internal (Alpha) Testing

Software testing is a process typically broken down into steps, based on how complete the coding of the program is. Testing a program typically begins in the company itself—the Alpha Test—and winds up in the hands of a select number of end-user guinea pigs—the Beta Test. In the early stages of testing, the program is put through its paces by the Quality Assurance (QA) team; in the later stages, when the program is more functional and more robust, it is used by people in the company who are representative of real-world users.

The Quality Assurance Team

In a sense, our careers in the commercial software development industry have paralleled the level of quality assurance involvement in the development process. In the early days—around 1986—at Peter Norton Computing there wasn't a dedicated QA team because we were such a small company. It was just us developers banging on each others' code. We didn't have a plan, other than thinking about what we could do to break someone else's code.

Over time, and through some experiences where we missed some heinous bugs, we discovered that more thought, more planning, and more personnel were required to adequately test the software we were developing. At first, this just meant involving more people within the company. The growing technical support team was doubling as our QA team. A dedicated, separate QA team was later put together. By the time we were developing the Norton Desktop for Windows, we had a state-of-the-art, fully staffed, fully functional QA team and equipment lab.

It was around this time—1990—that Symantec purchased Peter Norton Computing. Interestingly enough, our approach to QA was very similar to Symantec's approach, so little changed when Symantec acquired us—other than getting more people and more equipment so we could adequately test the software. More resources, along with better communications systems—primarily in the form of enterprise-wide e-mail—greatly enhanced our QA capabilities.

Borland's approach to QA had apparently taken a similar course. When the company was smaller, the testing was, by today's standards, pretty liberal. As the company and its products grew, so did its dedication to quality assurance. By the time we joined Borland in 1991—which was around the time Borland acquired Ashton-Tate—QA had become an important entity within the company's organization.

Quality Assurance today is a discipline requiring highly skilled personnel with various levels of experience. Typically, the QA team mirrors the development team. At Borland, for example, a single programmer was responsible for each of the components of the program we were developing. There also was a single QA person dedicated to each of the program's components. There was a one-to-one relationship between the developer and the tester. This was good because it allowed a close, very efficient means of checking the development of the component through its various stages.

The QA team is led by a manager, similar to the development manager heading the development team. The QA team manager oversees all aspects of the testing process and personnel. She or he keeps track of the testing's progress, and is responsible for ensuring the level of quality of the product being tested is as high as possible.

The individual members of the QA team, like the members of the development team, typically have varying levels of experience. They are responsible for the test's design, the actual testing of the software itself, and for keeping track of the bugs—the number, severity level, its state (whether it's been fixed or not), among other things. They typically will work together with the developer to find and remove as many bugs from the program as possible.

It is unfortunate that as developers, many of us take an adversarial approach to the QA team members. Perhaps, given the nature of their job—to uncover weakness in the programs we develop, which we often interpret as personal weakness—it is understandable that this occurs. However, this is far from beneficial to the development of robust programs.

As developers, we should know there will be bugs in the software we write. No matter how confident we are that the code we've written is robust, there's generally something we've either overlooked or are unaware of. It is the QA team's responsibility to uncover these anomalies in the code. We should be happy the QA team, and not the end user, finds these bugs.

An incredible amount of hard work and dedication go into software testing. For its part, the QA team needs to be aware an enormous amount of hard work and dedication go into software development. This is why our egos are often so highly involved with the work we do, and why it is difficult when someone discovers problems in the work that's been done. As developers, we shouldn't feel we've failed, but rather there's a problem that needs to be fixed. Once we and the QA team remove our egos from the process, the end result is that there's a bug someone found in the code, and it needs to be fixed before the product is shipped. By working together, the developer and tester can ensure the product being produced is the highest quality.

Initial Testing

At the companies where we've worked, software testing begins as soon as feasible, usually far from when the entire program is complete. The more testing that can be done, the better the probability bugs will be uncovered and fixed before the product is shipped.

It's been our experience that the Quality Assurance team is involved with the project from the beginning. In order to properly test the software, a plan must be developed, so knowledge about the project at its various stages is crucial to the program testing. At the early stages of the project, the QA team is primarily concerned with knowing what's coming its way, and when. As the project's code is developed, it begins to concern itself more and more with the hands-on software testing. Test plans are designed, test suites are developed, and test scripts are written. When the program is completed, its full force is unleashed and the program is put through its paces.

While the program is being developed, often the QA team will do initial, sometimes informal, testing of the code. This usually consists of ensuring that the basic functionality is there and the program works as expected. Since the program's interface typically is developed first, this is usually the first area tested. The results of activating the interface elements—the menu items, buttons, toolbar icons, and the like—are compared against what is expected to happen, usually from the Functional Spec. While some of the interface elements are functionally complete, most are not. But as long as there's an indication—perhaps through an alert box—of what is expected to happen when the element is activated, the basic works of the element can be ensured.

Beneath the interface's surface are the program's engines—the code that handles interaction and communication with the operating system, storage and retrieval of data, and perhaps transferral of data with another program, among other things. While the full functionality of these engines can't be tested until the entire program is complete, during the initial testing phase it is possible to ensure these engines perform their basic functionality as expected.

As a part of the Norton Desktop for Windows we wanted to enable the user to maintain his or her existing Program Manager groups—and the items in those groups—within our Quick Access program. We needed to write some code to read ProgMan's group files, and create our own Quick Access groups. The full functionality of this part of the program meant we'd be able to read the group files, separate the data found in there so it had meaning for us, internally create our own groups, then save a Quick Access group file.

Since this code was to be developed in stages, beginning with reading the group files, this is the first thing that could be tested. The code to do this was written, with hooks needed later for the code handling the interpretation of the data and subsequent storage into Quick Access group files. The initial draft of this program part merely reported what it encountered, a dump of the data stored in a file.

Once we were confident the program worked—at least as we'd expected it to—we handed it over to the QA team to test. It went through its own Program Manager group files to see if the program behaved. It tried it on group files throughout the computers at our location, then with some of its friends and colleagues outside the company. There were a few unexpected results, which were rapidly fixed. We were able to ensure the basic engine of the program worked as expected, long before the program was entirely complete.

Planning for the Test

As more of the program is completed, obviously more of it can be tested. But just as the software needs to have a design, so does the testing. Back in the early days of Peter Norton Computing, we simply banged on the software until we could find ways to break it. In effect, it's not much different from what's done in fully equipped QA departments. The major difference is that the banging has a design, it has a purpose, and it's not improvised.

The QA team ensures the product going out the door is as bug-free as possible. This means ways have to be devised to uncover bugs, particularly those hidden, sometimes highly damaging bugs caused by unexpected interactions with other software, be it the operating system or another program.

Starting from the Functional Spec, each of the software components is broken out and ways to test the code are devised. Each of the interface elements is tested for robustness. The limits of input to interface elements—text edit controls, for example—need to be ensured; their boundary conditions are tested. From the Functional Spec it is known how many characters can be entered into the text edit control, so the control needs to be tested for zero characters, less than the maximum number of characters, exactly the maximum number of characters, and finally, more than the maximum number of characters. Each of the pieces of the various components of the overall program must be tested in such a manner. A plan of attack is designed, concentrating on the boundary conditions, to ensure the program works as expected.

The component testing often can be automated, through macro recorders and test scripting programs. In recent years there have been a few automatic testing tools developed to assist in this process. Macro programs are used to record interaction with the interface—selecting in sequence each of the menu items, for instance—that later can be played back on other computers, with a report of the results automatically generated. This saves time and ensures the software is being reliably tested, because simply going through and activating the interface elements is tedious work, with a high level of fatigue involved with it. By automating this, QA personnel are freed up for other, more important—and less automatic—testing.

The capabilities of macro recorders are limited, however, so this is where testing scripts can be of help. Elaborate usage of the software often is required for the testing, but this is still something that can be automated, freeing up QA personnel for other activities. Testing scripts automate simulated user interaction with the operating environment. For example, what happens when the user launches other programs in the background while our program is involved in a lengthy file-saving operation? Again, this is a routine, tedious task for people to perform, but one fully suited to software.

By knowing what can be automated and what cannot, the resources of the QA team are used to their maximum. There are obviously areas of testing a program that involve human reasoning and problem-solving capabilities that are beyond automation, at least for now. So, by going through and looking at what the program is composed of, and what results are expected from these components, a design for testing the software—be it automatic or manual—can be devised. And it is with this design that the full robustness of the program can be established.

Usability Testing

One area of testing that has become more prominent in recent years involves the question of how effective the program's user interface is. By effective, we mean how readily is the user able to understand how to use the interface? What does the user expect from the interface, both as a whole and from its individual components? One way of determining the answers is to allow people to test the interface and provide feedback on what they encountered.

There are several usability testing companies located throughout the United States and the world. These are fully equipped labs, which provide a state-of-the-art facility for testing users' reactions to software interfaces. Many commercial software development companies have used these services in the past. Keep in mind that software testing can take several forms and can be applied at various stages of the product's development. Just like any other bug, the earlier problems in the interface can be found, the earlier they can be removed.

These bugs typically take the form of a user misunderstanding the interface's functionality. Increasingly so, focus groups—groups of 5 to 20 or more people—are gathered to examine a program's initial interface design. Just as market researchers test new product packaging, various designs and prototypes are created, and the one that gets the best result is used. Typically what is desired is an interface that is attractive, easy to understand, and easy to use. Through focus groups it is possible to debug the design of the interface long before it has been implemented, with an enormous savings of time and money.

After the program's interface has been implemented, the QA team ensures the application behaves as expected. At this stage of development, the program's interface is also tested from a more subjective viewpoint, one that seeks to ensure the interface is easy to understand and easy to use. People are gathered together to individually use the software and report back their feelings about the interface. This can be done in either a controlled setting—within a lab, for instance—or can be farmed out to people in various geographical locations. In the lab setting, there typically are video cameras that record various aspects of a user's interaction with the software.

Some labs are simply a conference room outfitted with a home video camera on a tripod aimed at a user sitting at a computer terminal. This method was actually used at Borland during the development of Quattro Pro for Windows. Quick feedback during initial development was necessary, so that's why testing was done in this fashion.

The more involved, more professional labs are equipped with multiple professional video cameras aimed at the user's hands—recording keyboard and mouse input, for example—and their faces—to record their emotional reactions as they use the program's interface—sometimes even a full-body shot used to indicate how comfortable people are when they use the software—a rapidly bouncing knee might be indicative of a stressful reaction to the interface, for example. The final interface testing of Quattro Pro for Windows was done by a professional lab in just this way. Some labs even have the capability of electronically tracking a user's emotional response to the software, in a fashion similar to what is used for lie detector tests.

All these tools can uncover problems a typical user might encounter in the interface. By identifying these interface problems as early as possible, less effort—along with time and money—will be expended on implementing an ineffective interface. And if this is postponed until after the program has been completed, it can have catastrophic results on when the program is actually shipped.

One of the strongest lessons we learned at Peter Norton Computing regarding this was when we redesigned the Norton Utilities for DOS, version 5.0. Up until this redesign, the programs consisted of a command-line interface, with its associated, arcane command-line switches used to tell the programs what to do. This made it very difficult and time-consuming for novices to use the software because they had to learn what switches to use to get done what they wanted. We redesigned the programs to have a friendlier interface, one that was easier for novice users to understand.

We were still a relatively small company then, so our usability testing was almost entirely limited to people within the company itself. As developers we were so concerned with making the programs easy for novices to use we'd forgotten about our core users—long-time users of the Norton Utilities who'd mastered using the command-line switches and were extremely adept at efficiently using the programs.

It turned out that when we shipped the nearly complete program to a select number of users for testing, one of the first results we got back from them was how slow and tedious the programs were to use. These testers were technically savvy users of the programs, not the novices we'd focused the interface redesign on. It was quickly realized that we couldn't ship something that was going to aggravate and alienate a large number of our users, so we had to go back and make the command-line versions of the programs more accessible by the experienced user. We'd been so concerned with how to make the programs easier for novices to use, we'd overlooked the fact we'd made them more difficult for experienced users! As a result of not learning this until the later stages of development, the program was shipped a little later—about a month—than we'd anticipated.

Alpha Testing

Officially, when all the product's features have been fully implemented, the Alpha test cycle can begin. While all the features are fully coded, their functionality cannot be guaranteed to work as expected. During the Alpha cycle the program's functionality is put to the test.

From a developer's standpoint, the Alpha test is an important milestone in the schedule. It is the point at which the majority of the coding has been completed. Theoretically, if we've done our jobs well enough, there won't be many bugs in our code. In actual practice, however, this isn't the case, so we'll be changing the code, making fixes to ensure it works properly. As we make these changes, the rest of the program is checked to make sure the changes made didn't break other areas of the program.

From a tester's standpoint, the Alpha test represents the first opportunity for using the program in its entirety. All features are accessible and testable, so interactions within the program as a whole can be examined. The Alpha test cycle typically begins within the QA team. It will utilize the test plan it devised, along with various tools, including automatic testing, to kick the software's tires, to make sure it works and doesn't break.

Once the program has gone through the QA team's grinder, it typically is released to select Alpha testers within the company. Often they are executives—mainly because they're interested in tracking the progress of the software first-hand—and a few workers in the company representative of real-world users. For example, with Quattro Pro for Windows, Borland's spreadsheet program, a group in the Finance department began using a very early Alpha version of the software as an initial step of verifying it worked in the business environment. As expected, there were places in the program that crashed, or hung, or where nothing happened at all. But it was important that these people were involved in the testing because in some cases they validated bugs already encountered by the QA team, and in other cases found ways of stretching the program so far it broke. (This doesn't mean the QA team failed; in the fast-paced, highly competitive world of commercial software development, only so much can be thought of in advance. There just isn't enough time to fully test all the boundaries of a program. That is why the Alpha and Beta test cycles are so important, and such a crucial part of the testing process.)

The Alpha cycle typically lasts anywhere from four to eight weeks, depending on the complexity of the application. This is what we've encountered for the programs we've worked on. For more complex programs—like operating systems—the Alpha cycle may last several months, and typically also includes testers from outside the company. In the case of operating systems, their complexity is extreme, as is their need to have a deeper, longer lasting test than is typically required of most commercial applications being developed.

Rating the Bugs

One of the most important aspects of a bug from a developer's standpoint is what kind of impact the bug has on the usability of the program. A bug has a level of severity—in effect, how badly it has broken the program—used by the developer as a means of prioritizing and categorizing the bugs. At the companies where we've worked, a system of four severity levels was utilized: Catastrophic, Severe with no work around, Severe with a work around, and Cosmetic. These are usually labeled levels "A" through "D" respectively. Other severity levels are used by other companies, with varying numbers of levels.

Catastrophic bugs are usually considered the bugs that cause a data loss, crash the program, or hang the operating system. Obviously these are the bugs that can have the worst impact and the ones that simply cannot go out in the shipping product. These have the highest priority for being fixed.

Severe bugs are not as bad as Catastrophic bugs in that they don't crash the system or cause a data loss, but they do indicate a feature doesn't behave or work as expected. They encompass two extremes: ones without a work around—the more severe—and ones with a work around. A *work around* means there is another way to accomplish the task, or to get the feature to work and behave as expected. This can either be through another feature, or by tweaking the use of the program in some manner. Typically, level "B" bugs—those without work arounds—are not acceptable in a shipping product, while some level "C" bugs are. These level "C" bugs are typically the types of bugs—along with any incompatibilities the software might have with some hardware—you'll see identified in a program's ReadMe file. Often there just isn't time to fix some of the lower-level "C" bugs by the time the product is to ship. Although this shouldn't be the case, most users are tolerant of these types of bugs, and in a way, sort of expect them in the initial release of a program. They are also some of the first things fixed for the next—often called "maintenance" or "bug-fix"—release of the program.

Interestingly enough, although the severity level of Cosmetic bugs is rather low, their tolerance in the shipping product is often lower than level "C" bugs. This is because the "C" bugs are often hidden underneath the surface of the program, whereas the Cosmetic bugs—misalignment of interface elements, and spelling errors in the text, for example—are very easy for the end user to find. And the more bugs a user finds—regardless of their severity level—the worse the impression the user is going to have of the software as a whole. It also helps that these are often the easiest bugs to fix. That is why a typical shipping program will have very few known level "D" bugs in it.

Bug Tracking Systems

Up until the Alpha cycle, bugs are usually tracked only on an informal basis. One of the reasons for this is that the code changes so much during development it's pretty much a waste of time to keep track of all the bugs encountered prior to the Alpha test. Most of them are irrelevant by the time the Alpha test begins. With the onset of the Alpha cycle, more bugs will be uncovered, and hence need to be accounted for.

A typical bug tracking system needs to identify what the bug is, how it was encountered, who found it, what hardware and operating system version were used, and the status of the bug—whether it's been fixed or not. Just as the QA process itself became more mature over time at the companies where we've worked, so have the bug tracking systems.

In the early days at Peter Norton Computing, our bug tracking system was pretty much nonexistent. It consisted of handwritten notes to each other about bugs encountered. It was up to the developer to make sure the bugs got fixed. Given the small number of people on the team, and the nature of the code we were writing at the time, this was a reasonable approach, and it worked fairly well.

As the company grew, the development team also grew, as did the complexity of the software we were writing. The next stage in the evolution of our bug tracking system was a paper-based form used to keep track of information about the bugs encountered. This was an initial way of organizing the bugs in a useful manner.

One of the limitations of this paper-based system was that it was difficult to track the bugs' progress. Finding and modifying a single bug report was not an easy process, so often it wasn't done. Many of the bugs indicated as not having been fixed yet on the form were in fact fixed a long time before.

The next stage in the bug tracking system's evolution was to put it into a computer database. This way we could easily find and keep track of individual bugs and their progress. We also could get rudimentary reports about the number and severity of bugs. By knowing how many "A" and "B" bugs we had, we could better estimate when we were really going to ship the product, which greatly enhanced our marketing and manufacturing efforts.

By the time the Norton Desktop for Windows was being developed, we had a fully functioning bug system accessible by the developers themselves. This greatly enhanced the efficiency of our bug fixing capabilities because we could rapidly get a report and categorization of bugs, and quickly access the details of specific bugs. It was also easier for us to keep track of the state of the bugs because we had direct access to the reports.

Bugs are typically assigned a status used to indicate if the bug needs to be fixed, and if the bug is "Open" or "Closed." Open bugs usually are considered to be those bugs the developer has not yet fixed. By fixing, we mean that not only has the programmer made alterations to the code as a means of eliminating the bug, but also that the change has been verified by the QA team. "Open" bugs can consist both of bugs yet to be fixed by the programmer, and those that have been fixed, but not yet verified by the QA team.

Once a bug fix has been verified, it can be moved into the "Closed" category. Other types of bugs in this category include bugs that couldn't be reproduced, bugs labeled "As Designed," and other irrelevant or erroneous bugs. "As Designed" bugs are bugs where the tester anticipated one action but the program did another, which is the "correct" action according to the design. It also may be the case where an unexpected limitation of the program is encountered. These bugs are important to track, because they are often indicative of flaws in the design—be it the interface design or the program's internal architecture. It's usually a good idea when development of the next version of the program begins to reexamine these "As Designed" bugs because it's an excellent opportunity to rethink the design of the program.

By tracking the Open and Closed status of bugs, an indication of the probability the product will ship can be gained. For example, if according to the schedule you're supposed to ship in two weeks and you've got 500 open bugs, the likelihood that you're actually going to ship a robust product is pretty slim. It's scary to think, but there are rumors that some products have knowingly gone out the door with well over 100 high-priority bugs in them. Management decided that it was better to ship something in a reasonable time frame than to get a fully completed product out late. And unfortunately, the end-user community has been pretty powerless to oppose this situation, other than to expect—and sometimes demand—free upgrades to the finished, fully functional product when it's available.

Borland's bug tracking was the most highly developed, most capable bug tracking system we've encountered. A Paradox application, based on Borland's successful database program, was utilized on the network throughout the company. All the products being developed at Borland relied on this program to keep track of the product's bugs. It was an elaborately detailed program, with a wide assortment of reporting capabilities. One of the most useful was a chart that indicated the rate at which bugs were being found and how quickly they were being fixed. This was again useful for tracking the probability of the product being shipped on schedule.

This bug tracking program was developed and maintained internally by a Borland group. As is the case with any custom program, a fairly large development effort went into producing the program. When it was developed, however, there were few, if any, off-the-shelf bug tracking programs available. Today there are several programs available commercially to track bugs in software.

Beta Testing

When the Alpha cycle ends—at least according to the schedule—an examination of the number and severity of bugs is made, and from this it typically is determined if the Beta cycle can begin. Technically speaking, the Beta cycle is officially entered when the code is pretty much frozen: not only are the features completed, but they should work and behave as expected. The changes to the code should be minimal, so the impact on the overall product can be contained.

As is often the case in commercial software development, at least at the companies where we've worked, there is a bit of negotiability in the semantics of the Alpha and Beta test cycles. The realities of shipping commercial software dictate this. If we had gone by the book as far as what exactly was software ready for Alpha and Beta testing, the products we developed would have been months late, with little or no benefit as far as actual, perceivable quality was concerned. The statistics might have looked a bit better, but the typical end user would have noticed little or no impact on the product because of this.

This isn't to say, however, the Alpha and Beta cycles can be approached in a relaxed manner. This was never the case. It was just that there was an understanding between the development and QA teams of exactly what was expected from the product as we entered the testing cycles.

As an example, not every single feature of the Norton Desktop for Windows was fully coded when we entered the Alpha stage of the program. Officially—according to the book—we shouldn't have entered the Alpha stage. But because there were so many individual components and features in the program that could be tested independently of each other, it was silly to hold up the overall schedule of the product for semantic reasons. What was done, in effect, was stretch out the entry time of the Alpha cycle, so the finished parts could be attacked first, while the development of the other pieces was completed. Because there was an understanding and communication between the development and QA teams, this had virtually no impact on the timely shipping of the product. It would have been a waste of QA time to simply wait until we were "officially" done with all of the program and could begin the Alpha cycle.

In the case of the Norton Desktop for Windows—because of the high level of departmentalization—it was reasonable to enter the Alpha cycle, even though all the components hadn't been fully coded yet. To a certain extent this leniency towards the rule-book definition carried over into the Beta cycle, but again it was manageable because the QA team was well aware of what needed testing.

Stages of Beta Testing

As with the Alpha cycle, typically the Beta cycle is gradually unleashed on a larger and larger number of testers. It begins within the QA team, where the Beta status is confirmed. If the program breaks unexpectedly and rather easily in too many places, it would be a waste of time to release the program to a large pool of testers, where a large number of bugs need to be tracked. It would in effect defeat the purpose of the Beta cycle, where it is desired that the user uncover those hard to find, rather deeply hidden bugs that crop up when the program is used in real-world situations.

Fortunately enough, it is rarely the case that seriously broken software is sent into Beta test. This is mainly because the progress of the program's quality is tracked as it is being developed. There have been a few instances, however, where individual components of the programs we've worked on have unexpectantly broken at the beginning of the Beta cycle, and needed to be fixed before the product could be tested by a large number of outside testers.

When the quality of the program is deemed relatively high, a group of seed users—what is commonly known as the Beta testers—is provided with a copy of the program and its documentation and begin the real-world program testing. Again, depending on the complexity of the application, the number of Beta testers can range from the hundreds to the tens of thousands. Surprisingly enough, some software manu-facturers even charge for their Beta software. Remember the initial OS/2 development kits? They were around two thousand bucks a pop. Of course, you got a bookshelf's worth of documentation and a godzillion diskettes used to install the operating system.

Charging to use Beta software is the exception to the rule, however. (Although, given the nature of software that has sometimes been shipped in the past, what is supposed to be a final version of the prod-uct is, in actual fact, nothing more than an advanced Beta version of the program.) When a charge for Beta software is made, typically the carrot at the end of the stick is that the user will get the final version of the product for a discount—or often at no charge at all.

For most Beta testers, the software is free—at least as far as money is concerned. But as with everything in this world, there is a price for using Beta software, and the price can be relatively high. As experienced Beta testers ourselves, we can tell you that it's important to make sure you have a robust backup system—or better yet, a separate system you can easily trash and not worry about—as a means of ensuring the integrity of your system's data. It is unfortunately rather easy for a program to inad-vertently destroy data in a user's system, so just in case this happens it's best to have a backup in hand.

Also, there can be a pretty high frustration level when using Beta soft-ware. Things don't always work as expected, and sometimes bugs are encountered at crucial moments, like when saving something you've been working on for a long time. And for the most part, doing proper Beta testing is not easy work. You've got to keep track of and report the bugs you encounter, which can be a time-consuming process. Most companies are now utilizing on-line services—either bulletin-board systems or commercial systems such as CompuServe—for their Beta testers to communicate the bugs they encounter. It's an efficient means in terms of time and money—both for the tester and the company—of keeping track of bugs.

This doesn't say that Beta testing software isn't fun at all. We've had the fortune to get first looks at some truly incredible pieces of software, some of which would have been very expensive had we purchased them ourselves. Typically the reward we've gotten for being a Beta tester is receiving a free copy of the final, shipping version of the program once it was completed, sometimes with a registration card that entitled us to reduced cost upgrades in the future. So although the work can sometimes be hard, the reward can more than compensate for the frustrations encountered in Beta software.

The typical Beta test cycle lasts anywhere from 12 to 18 weeks, again depending on the complexity of the software. As with Alpha software, highly complex applications—like operating systems—have longer Beta test periods, lasting anywhere from four to nine months or longer. One of the reasons for the longer time period for more complex software such as operating systems is that it is an application that will potentially be used on tens of millions of machines, so the probability that unexpected bugs will be encountered is much higher than if the software is eventually going to be used on "only" several hundred thousand systems.

Managing the Testers

Once the software is released into the hands of the Beta testers, the testing process isn't over. To a certain extent it's only really, fully, just begun. Up until this point, the software has been used in relatively controlled environments. Once it's unleashed into the real world, chaos may reign supreme. Unexpected interactions with other software, hardware, and operating systems will be encountered; and other, more deeply hidden areas of the software's code will be stressed. These typically will cause the program to break in ways that were not—often could not be— anticipated in advance.

Recruiting Testers

Obviously a successful Beta test program begins with a wide range of "typical" users who can be drawn upon to put the application through its paces. Building a pool of these users to be utilized during the Beta cycle is an important part of the overall testing process.

Many companies receive numerous requests from users to join the ranks of the Beta testers. They know of the rewards available, so the attraction of becoming a Beta tester can be rather compelling to many people. For the company, what they're looking for are people who can reliably test and report results of their tests back to the QA team. They're also interested in users with special capabilities—be it unusual hardware systems or elaborate software needs—who can test the program in important ways other testers can't provide. For example, with the Norton Desktop for Windows, we wanted to ensure the program would work on a wide number of networks, so we made sure we had people with these networks as part of our Beta program.

Many companies begin building their Beta lists with people they've used in the past, mainly because these are known, proven testers. If a particular capability is desired, many times the Technical Support department will be used to troll for potential Beta users. And some companies keep track of nearly everyone who expresses an interest in becoming a Beta tester, almost to the level they use for recruiting people to work for the company. Other companies have begun to utilize the on-line services as a means of determining valuable Beta testers, typically people who frequent the "forums" on the service, like CompuServe.

If you're interested in becoming a Beta tester, you might start by talking to someone in the Sales department. This is often the easiest part of the organization to get in touch with over the telephone. And unlike the Customer Service staff, the Sales people will likely have access to someone with the authorization of adding to the Beta list, like the Product Manager or the Quality Assurance Manager. Make yourself sound as important to the salesperson as possible; perhaps the sales person has a future, rather large order that may materialize because of you. Don't hide or sidestep what you're after. Be up front and honest, and let the salesperson know how his or her company can benefit from your Beta testing of its software. Be sure to accent your special capabilities for testing the software in unusual ways, be it your experience and knowledge of competing products, or special, unusual hardware configurations that can be used to test the software.

Depending on the size of the company you're dealing with, the salesperson may or may not be influential about who's added to the Beta test list. Usually, the larger the organization the more gyrations you're going to have to go through in order to get on the Beta list, although some of the largest companies have specialized, often direct, means of getting onto the list of Beta testers. With the smaller companies, however, it is fairly easy to get your name passed on to the right person so you can be added to the list. If you can, determine who's responsible for the list, and contact him or her directly, again trumpeting your special capabilities and experience in testing software. By making yourself an attractive potential tester you make it easier for the person or persons responsible for the Beta list to add your name.

Tracking the Testers

Once the program has been released to the Beta testers, it often is necessary to keep track of how well they are living up to their responsibilities. With some Beta testers, virtually no tracking is necessary because they are in constant contact with the company about the state of the program. With others, it is necessary to contact them and obtain the results of their tests.

Keeping track of and contacting individual Beta testers can be an expensive and time-consuming process. That is why many companies are now automating this process through on-line services. Electronic bug reporting forms are used so the user can easily communicate bugs as they are encountered. Direct-access bulletin board systems dedicated to the Beta testers are another means of making the process easier.

When users must be individually contacted to track their progress, it can be a nightmare. Both at Peter Norton Computing and at Borland, many of the testers we used weren't as reliable at communicating their results as we'd have liked. It was necessary to get in contact with these people—both by mail and through telephone calls—and obtain their test results. In the Norton Desktop for Windows' case, this entailed having several people dedicated to this communication process. This was no easy task, but one that was necessary for the program's success.

When a Beta tester isn't providing you with the feedback you need, you probably want to remove that person from the Beta testing process and find another, more reliable person. We had to do this for a few people while Beta testing the Norton Desktop for Windows. The people were given a few chances to respond to our queries—both written and by telephone. If, after three telephone calls, we still hadn't received the feedback we'd expected about the test, a final call was made to notify the person that his or her status as a Beta tester had been cancelled. We kept a list of alternate testers, so we went to that list and recruited a new Beta tester.

If you ever become a Beta tester, please be aware you are providing a valuable service for the company for which you are testing the software. Take this responsibility to heart and try to live up to it. Sometimes the systems the company has in place will aid you in this; other times they will get in the way. If you encounter problems communicating results back to the company, let someone know, so the problem can be fixed. If you find you can't stand to use the program, be honest and have your name taken off the list. If you don't like the Beta version
of the program enough to test it, you more than likely won't like the finished version any better. And what use is software you won't utilize in the future? It's better to be honest and tell the company its program is bad, why it's bad, and why you don't want to do any more testing of the product, than to simply not say anything and let the test period elapse.

Beta Test Leaks

One of the unfortunate aspects of having Beta testers is not being able to effectively control how much information they release about the program to other people before this information is made available to the public. One of the barriers to users simply blabbing about the software they're testing is the *Non-Disclosure Agreement* (NDA). This legally binding document limits what the tester can discuss about the product with other people outside the company or Beta test program. Typically the NDA rather flatly says nothing about the program can be discussed, or disseminated in any manner, to anyone outside the company.

Typically the secrecy in the testing program is for competitive reasons. You don't want your competitor to have too close a look at your product before its shipping, for a couple of reasons. The first is it will likely get ideas about how to enhance an existing product—or build a new one from scratch—to compete against your program. The second is that the competitor may be able to develop an effective marketing campaign that takes the wind out of your sails before or just as you announce and release the program to the public. In either case, sales of your program can be affected, so great caution has to be taken to ensure Beta testers don't leak information to your competitors.

Actually enforcing an NDA is a difficult process and has many legal concerns. But without the NDA there would be few, if any, legal courses of action. The threat of liability is a necessary fact in the business world. For the most part the NDA is an unnecessary document because the majority of Beta testers are honest and will live up to the spirit of their commitment to testing the software with or without an NDA. But protection against competitors, as well as counterfeiters, is essential, so you may choose to establish an NDA after all.

Some leaks actually can be beneficial. When we were developing the initial version of the Norton Desktop for Windows, for instance, a high level of secrecy and security was maintained because our strategy was geared towards our product being the only viable solution to an integrated file and data management program for Windows. We'd pretty much maintained that security throughout the development process. However, during the Beta test period the press got hold of an early Beta version of the program, either directly or indirectly through the Beta test program. Fortunately it was robust enough, and rich enough feature-wise that the press accounting was in effect an advertisement for our product. And because it was so late in the development of the product, there was little our competitors could do to counter our program in a short time span.

Feedback to Developers

One of the essential aspects of software testing is ensuring the developers are routinely updated with the status of their projects. One way this is implemented is through the bug tracking system. Another is through the organization's communications systems, the phone, and e-mail systems. Another is through periodic meetings of the QA team and the development team. For the bugs to be fixed, the developers must be aware of them and their status.

Communication through the Bug Tracking System

Feedback is routinely sent to the developer through the bug tracking system. As bugs are encountered—through internal or external testers—the reports are entered into the bug tracking system. Each bug is assigned a unique ID, given a severity level, and typically assigned to the developer responsible for implementing the code in the module in which the bug has been found. In this manner, an individual programmer can scan the system for a listing of his or her bugs.

When a bug is fixed, the programmer can indicate that a given version of the program attempts to fix the problem. The QA team then can verify if the bug is in fact fully fixed and that it has no known impact on the rest of the program. If for any reason the fix isn't complete, the bug will remain open and in need of being repaired. If the fix does actually work, then the bug can be closed.

One of the most important aspects of the bug tracking system, at least for the developer, is being able to accurately re-create the bug. If it's a bug that can't be replicated, the job of fixing the bug is usually impossible. (In some, typically rare, cases the fix for the bug is so obvious that no replication is necessary.) Usually the hardware the program was used on and the operating system version it was used under are provided as a means of identifying any special incompatibilities that may be encountered.

A detailed accounting of the steps taken to encounter the bug is provided so the bug can be replicated—first by the developer to be able to fix it, then later by the QA team to verify the bug is really fixed. Verifying the bug fix is sometimes a difficult thing to do, because of the intricacies involved in causing the bug to occur, or because there isn't enough room on the form to fully explain all the steps that led to the bug.

Often, the reports are ambiguous, incomplete, or muddied. In these cases, the developer makes an indication—either on the form itself, or directly to the tester—that it's not clear how to replicate the bug. The tester can then clarify the steps necessary to duplicate the bug.

In some cases the steps may be clearly labeled, but when they are taken, the bug is not encountered by the developer. It may be the latest version of the program the developer is using inadvertently fixes the bug. It also may be the bug was an aberration limited to a one-time encounter on the tester's system, or perhaps limited to the hardware and operating system on the tester's system. In either case, bugs that the developer cannot reproduce are indicated as such. These bugs then are typically tested on yet another system by another tester, and if the bug is encountered again, it's bounced back to the developer. Otherwise, it may be tried again on the original system. If it doesn't come up again, it's likely a one-time event that was somehow encountered. If it does come up again, it's likely something specific to that tester's system, so the developer will be informed as such.

Utilizing the Organization's Communications Systems

Because of its capabilities, a typical bug tracking system is the most efficient means to routinely communicate and update the bugs encountered. There are occasions, however, when other means of providing feedback to the developers is necessary. Special circumstances are encountered on some occasions, and it would be difficult, perhaps impossible, to adequately communicate this through the bug tracking system.

The bug tracking system typically is utilized as a kind of bulletin board where the bugs are posted and the developers can access them at will. In some circumstances, a bulletin board approach to this communication is inadequate and other communications systems within the company must be used.

This typically involves utilizing communications systems that allow the tester direct access to the developer, and this access is usually limited to internal testers. There are some special circumstances, however, where a small number of external testers can have direct communication with the developers. Sometimes, if a member of the press is having a particularly difficult time with a part of the program, the developer responsible for that piece is made available to work through the problem.

Direct access to the developer is usually facilitated through telephone, e-mail, or direct, face-to-face communication. It usually depends on the urgency of the bug as to what is used. If there isn't an urgency, and it easily can be explained in an e-mail message, it's an efficient means of communicating to the developer because the developer can access the message at his or her will, when the time is appropriate for them to do so.

Telephone calls and direct face-to-face communications are usually pretty disruptive to the development process, so these are kept to a minimum. Sometimes, as developers, we need to ignore any direct communications so we can get something with a special urgency done. Most companies have some sort of voice mail system, which provides the tester with a means to communicate to the developer what's going on, without disturbing the developer at perhaps a critical point.

Many companies provide individual offices for their developers, offices with doors that can be closed when necessary. This doesn't necessarily mean that disruption won't occur; it just is an indication by the programmer that he or she doesn't want to be disturbed for something that can wait. When the door is open, so is access to the developer. For developers in cubicles, the door is in effect always open, so it's difficult to limit direct access the same way an office door can. However, as a developer, it's up to you to know when you can and can't be disturbed, so on those occasions when you are disturbed—regardless of whether or not you're in an office—let the person interrupting you know that it's a bad time and that perhaps the issue can be dealt with at a later time, a time more convenient to you.

Communication through Meetings

A final means of communicating feedback to the developers is through meetings which typically involve the QA and programming teams. These usually are periodic meetings that during the initial stages of development and testing occur less frequently than at the later stages of the project.

At both Symantec and Borland, these meetings were usually every other week during the early stages of the project, and were often extremely short. Basically, the meetings were just reports provided by the developers about the status of the projects they were working on.

As the project developed, the meetings became increasingly longer—but not by too much—to accommodate the new levels of feedback provided by the QA team members. They reported the status of their aspect of the project as well, which accounted for the increased duration of the meetings.

When the program neared its later stages of development, and as the early stages of the testing process approached, the frequency of the meetings—and hence the importance of the meetings—was increased to once a week. These were again short meetings because it was primarily the developers indicating the status of the projects, about how close they were to being done.

During the later stages of the Beta cycle, the frequency of the meetings was increased to every day to maintain a high level of communication between the developers and the testers, as well as the managers responsible for the project. At Borland these were called "Bug Councils," and in them bugs were prioritized and a strategy for fixing them was developed. (We did a similar thing at Symantec/Peter Norton Computing, but didn't have a fancy name for it.)

Sometimes a Bug Council was a negotiating session, where at times the developers would say they could easily fix a bug, but others would veto the fix because its impact on the rest of the program couldn't be guaranteed. At other times it would be the developers saying that in order to fix a bug they'd need to re-implement something and there just wasn't time to do it correctly. In these cases, work arounds often were found to side-step the bug, at least in the initial version of the program. It would later be fixed in a correct manner and made available in a maintenance release.

The main benefit of these direct, frequent meetings between the developers and the testers was to ensure the product about to be shipped was as high quality as possible within a reasonable time frame.

Without the dedication and hard work of the Quality Assurance team members, the software we all use on a daily basis would be far less robust. Testing software requires a special kind of person, one who enjoys looking for ways the program can be stretched and bent to see if it breaks. As developers, we'd like to take this opportunity to thank all the people we've known over the years who have done such an excellent job of ensuring the quality of the software we've had the fortune of developing.

Conclusion

In this chapter we've taken an overview of the software quality assurance process. Just as the design and development of the product are done in an evolutionary manner, so is the quality assurance:

- The program is first tested by members of the Quality Assurance team.

- The Alpha Test by people within the company provides the next step in the quality assurance process.

- The Beta Test by a select group of people outside the company provides a real-world testing of the program.

- Communication with the Beta testers is essential in ensuring that the process is being adequately completed.

- When the program's quality is acceptable, the product is ready for manufacturing and shipment to end users.

Chapter 7

Software Documentation

This chapter gives you hints on writing software documentation. You learn about printed documentation and on-line help. Topics covered include choosing a document processing application, writing tutorials, creating help systems, and working with computer-based training systems. Furthermore, you gain an overview of tools available that can help you create online help.

This chapter covers the following topics:

- How to plan your documentation.

- How to organize and outline the material you want to include in your documentation.

- How to choose between a word processing or desktop publishing application for creating your documentation.

- Ideas on creating a good tutorial for your application. Information to help you decide if a tutorial is necessary.

- Information about computer-based training systems.

- Ideas and concepts you should be familiar with when writing on-line documentation.

- Tools for creating on-line help that use the WinHelp engine.

Creating Software Documentation

Before writing any documentation, you should plan its organization and content. At this time you can also plan the physical appearance of the documentation. Some of the things to keep in mind include:

- Will the documentation include a tutorial?

- What sort of reference information is required? How will it be organized?

- How should the documentation be organized? Into sections? Into chapters?

- How many bound manuals should the documentation be separated into? What logical manuals should be created?

- What sort of appendixes are necessary? What sort of reference material should be included in the manual?

- How will the printed manual correspond to the on-line help system?

- Will the printed documentation need to correspond to any tutorials included as part of your documentation?

When planning the physical appearance of documentation, things to ask yourself include:

- What font should be used?

- What will the margins be set to on the documents?

- How will headers and footers appear? Should the headers include chapter titles, page numbers, and section numbers?

- How will the document be printed? Will output on a laser printer be acceptable, or should it be sent to a linotronic to be printed at 1,200 dots per inch?

- How will tables be formatted?

- How will figures appear and how should they be referenced? Do you want to show full screen shots, or just images of specific dialog boxes?

- Will there be a table of contents? Will there be an index?

The success of your documentation depends on its usefulness. Many things contribute to the usefulness. Clarity is one important contributor. It begins with efforts to ensure every element is in its place, the right things are explained at the right times, and the needs of the audience—the people who bought your software—receive careful attention.

By answering the above questions, you are on your way to making your documentation useful, and therefore helpful to the customer.

Planning the Documentation

One of the easiest ways to plan your documentation is to create an outline for the manual. You should start with main chapter titles. Arrange the content so it progresses from simple concepts to more difficult ones. You should also make sure you think ahead of time about making the manual a handy reference to the software. After all, once the user has learned how to access the main features of the software but wants to find out about a specific concept, will the documentation still be useful?

Once you have selected chapter titles, break each chapter into sections. Make an outline for each chapter. Try to progress between topics in each chapter in a systematic manner. Try to start from beginning material and progress to more advanced material.

Having broken your subject outline into chapters, you can begin thinking about the introductions, transitions, and summaries that tie the sections and chapters together. If you need to break a major topic among chapters, then you should think about adding a section that explains what is covered in the current chapter, what is covered in the next chapter, and how the two are related.

Another contributing factor to your documentation's usefulness is easy access to information. No matter how much useful information your documentation contains, it will only gather dust unless the information is presented in such a way the reader can find what he or she needs with a minimum effort.

Some of the elements of documentation which can make information easier to access include:

- Chapter and section summaries to aid the reader in locating information.

- Subheadings to show the progression of topics.

- Lists and tables for quick summaries of important information.

- Figures and diagrams to present ideas in concrete form.

- Properly prepared indexes.

If you examine the documentation from the big boys and girls (Microsoft, Borland, Symantec, Lotus, and Novell), you probably will see other ideas that make the documentation easy to use. There are always new things that can be done. The ideas are just waiting to be discovered.

Writing the Documentation

The number of people working on a given manual depends on the size of the manual and how complex the software is to document. Borland has teams of 20 or 30 people working on manuals for some of its products. Of course this is probably expected for a product like Paradox for Windows which itself contains six separately bound books.

A small software company might have one or two people working entirely on the manual. In some ways, this can make the manual more cohesive and easier to use. It is a well-known fact that putting more people on a project does not necessarily increase the output of a group of writers.

Because documentation relies on technical facts, writers must be in constant communication with other people on the team, especially the developers who are creating the application. The writers must know how a feature works and what it is for. It would also help for the writer to know why a feature was implemented in a certain way. This helps the writer explain how the feature works. It is always nice to know *about* a certain feature, but it is more helpful to know *how* to use a certain feature in real life situations.

Working with Schedules

One of the most difficult aspects of the software industry is that deadlines on large programming projects are often missed. Projects get delayed by months, maybe even years, and products change in the process.

> **Note**
>
> I think the award for the software product that was most delayed was Lotus 1-2-3 for the Macintosh. It was delayed by something like seven years from the originally promised ship date.
>
> Second place for the software product that has been delayed the longest goes to Microsoft for its delayed introduction of Windows 3.1.

This is frustrating to everybody involved, but it can be especially difficult for those writing the documentation because they write that the software works a certain way. They go ahead and write about the specified feature(s). In the meantime the product specification changes, and all the written documentation that was already completed is thrown out the door (into the proverbial bit-bucket), and the writer needs to start over. Although this might be great for job security, as far as producing written documentation, the first effort was a total waste.

Last Minute Changes

Documentation authors so often must work way ahead of the deadline for the software because it takes much more time to print manuals than it does to create distribution disks. Historically, manuals are printed months before the software is completed. This results in the inevitable README.TXT file that comes on disk #1 of most software products.

Some users complain these readme files are a result of poor planning on the part of software companies. These same people think everything in the readme file should have been included in Chapter 1 of the user's manual. Although this may be true to a certain extent, it is just not possible—it's a part of the industry.

Because manuals must go to printers months before a product is due to ship, software developers are still working on features in the application when the documents are finalized. As a result, there often are changes to the software in these last final months of the development process. That is why some readme files end up being 20 or 30 pages long.

Updating Documentation

In *On Writing Well*, author William Zinsser, who is also the editor of
the Book-of-the-Month Club, says "the essence of writing is rewriting." Although he doesn't mention software documentation specifically, I think the same rule applies. I think it is a valuable tip to any
author. Zinsser himself believes strongly in this concept because his
entire book is based on it. The idea is to strip every sentence in your
manual to its cleanest components. In his book, Zinsser gives examples
of famous authors who rewrite their books four or five times.

In my own experience, I have found Zinsser's words extremely helpful.
Sometimes it is not easy to explain a software feature, so you go ahead
and type whatever comes to mind. The resulting words may not be
acceptable English. However, by modifying and rewriting the words
and sentences, you come up with something that explains the specified feature and does so in a clear and concise manner.

Hints on Grammar

You want to make sure a finished manuscript is free of grammatical
faults. You should have as many people look over the documentation
as possible. This includes everybody in your group (if you are in a large
company) or everybody in the company (if it is a small company). This
process also helps you find areas of the documentation that may not
be as well written as they could be.

The standard for grammatical style is probably set by the book
Elements of Style by William Strunk, Jr. and E.B. White (Macmillan
Publishing Co., Inc.). It is a short book written in 1959 and updated
in 1979 that tries to provide rules and principles for writers to follow.
I think most writers and editors agree that rereading it yearly keeps
them reminded of important rules that have helped many writers
through the years. Many colleges use the book as their guideline for
writing papers. I don't think it matters what type of writing you are
doing; this book will help you create a consistent style all readers will
appreciate.

Choosing a Document Processor

The obvious choice of document processor is selecting software you
already use and are familiar with. Technically, you can use any type of

document processor you desire. You should use a program with which you are familiar, especially with advanced features like headers, footers, style sheets, table of contents creation, and index marking.

The term *document processor* is used here to refer to both word processors and desktop publishing programs. In the past, word processors were used for writing purely textual-based documents and desktop publishing programs were used to create any document that had a graphical element. That is no longer true.

The distinction between word processor and desktop publishing program has been blurred. Using a graphical word processor like Word for Windows, you can now accomplish most of the things that would have required a desktop publishing program like PageMaker several years ago. The choice of which to use is really up to you. You should make the decision based on what software you are already using, and what type of page layout features you need.

Common word processors you might choose from include: WordPerfect (for DOS or for Windows) or Microsoft Word (for DOS or for Windows). Although Word for Windows allows you to work with graphics and layout designs much more fluently than its DOS counterpart, I know a publisher who prefers Word for DOS because it provides a much more intuitive and easily accessible environment. Word for DOS is also faster than its Windows-based sibling.

Common desktop publishing programs include PageMaker, QuarkXPress, FrameMaker, and Ventura Publisher. Situations when you might prefer using a desktop publishing program over a word processor would be when you need specialized wrapping of text around a figure or features that are not available in your word processor. Many professionals who specialize in desktop publishing use desktop publishing programs in conjunction with word processors. The word processors are used for writing and rewriting the document. The text is then placed into the desktop publishing program for altering figures.

Generally, the physical appearance of your manuscript can be fairly simple. You shouldn't try to overdo the look of the documentation with lots of fancy fonts. Basic elements of any documentation include a header and footer (including page numbers), two or three layers of headline titles, and the body text.

> **Note**
>
> Borland uses its very own Sprint word processor for all in-house documentation. Although it was not much of a market success, Sprint is still used to maintain a good portion of its documentation. However, as new products were acquired, the related documentation was often in various word processing formats, so the company now uses several word processing standards. Although Sprint is difficult to use, it was preferred because it excelled at quickly handling large documents.
>
> I am sure that internally, Microsoft uses Word as its document processor of choice, and along the same line, WordPerfect Corporation uses its own WordPerfect document processor (and if it doesn't already, Novell will be using WordPerfect very soon, also). It would be silly not to. Not only does it save the cost of software, but using its application in-house gives it valuable ideas on how to update and add new features to the product in the future.

Tutorials

To get users up and running with your application as soon as possible you may consider providing a tutorial. The tutorial should provide step-by-step instructions for showing the user how to use and access the major features of your application.

A tutorial usually includes printed documentation with steps the users follow. It also has data files on disk that the user accesses to complete the tutorial. This is hands-on learning at its best. Many people believe it provides the best way to learn something new, second only to having
a private teacher sit next to you and lead you every step of the way (which is impractical in many situations).

If you are going to provide a tutorial, make sure you coordinate with other people at your company to ensure any necessary tutorial data files are included on the distribution disks.

Some popular software that provides tutorials includes:

- Paradox for Windows
- Quattro Pro for Windows

- Visual C++ (a tutorial to the Microsoft Foundation Classes)

- Borland C++ (a tutorial to the ObjectWindows Library)

The most identifying aspect of a tutorial is the fact that the user usually reads the product manuals and follows steps identified in the manual using data provided on disk.

For example, the tutorial that comes with Visual C++ has six steps outlined in ten chapters; it takes the user (who in this case is a programmer) through using Visual C++ utilities (AppWizard, ClassWizard, and AppStudio) for creating a starter application. It starts by showing the user how to create a minimum MFC-based application and it brings that user through the following steps: creating document files, working with application views, accessing menus and toolbars, creating message handlers, creating dialog boxes, scrolling and splitting windows, printing and print preview features, and providing context-sensitive help.

The Visual C++ tutorial requires about 188 pages of documentation along with 5 megabytes of source code included on disk. You can see a tutorial of this complexity requires lots of planning and coordinating between writers and programmers alike.

Research has shown tutorials provide an effective method of getting the user up to speed on an application.

Computer-Based Training

Computer-based training (CBT) is a series of tutorials that guide the user through the steps of using an application. In computer-based training systems, there is rarely any printed documentation to provide additional help. Everything is provided on-line.

The study of computer-based training is still in its infancy. Companies are searching for ways to make learning software easier. Many of the big companies have departments (or have had departments at one time) the sole purpose of which is to find out how to develop and create computer-based training systems.

Examples of available computer-based training systems include:

- Microsoft Windows 3.1 (accessed from Program Manager)

- Microsoft Visual Basic

You find computer-based training to be more difficult to add to a software product than tutorials, because computer-based training requires programmers who are trained at teaching people how to learn something. They must then write a program that shows users how to use a product as well as come up with a way to teach people the product.

Another difficulty with computer-based training is that if the product changes substantially, the tutorial must be rewritten. This requires constant attention to the creation and updating of computer-based training systems.

I don't know how most companies write their computer-based training programs, but Windows does provide certain hooks into the operating system that makes creating these systems easier.

A good computer-based training program includes:

- Showing how to carry out a specified action.

- Allowing the user to carry out the action, and making sure he or she carries it out correctly.

- Making the training interactive, so the user always knows if he or she is learning correctly.

- Providing visual cues so the user knows he or she is doing the right thing.

- Providing review lessons to make sure the user learned the suggested topic.

- Including follow-up questions to make sure the user learned the specified topics.

You can see that there is certainly a lot to writing a computer-based training system. Not only must you have programmers who can create a cohesive program, but they must also be good at writing tutorials, and teaching people (through the use of the computer) how a program operates.

The big question remains if computer-based training is effective. Implementing this sort of training certainly requires more work. In many circumstances computer-based training programs provide beginner lessons designed to get the neophyte user up and running quickly.

A perfect example is the computer-based training that comes with
Windows 3.1. It provides information about using a mouse and interacting with Windows only a neophyte could appreciate. Anybody who
can use a mouse or type on a keyboard will find the tutorial boring.

> **Tip**
>
> To access the Windows 3.1 computer-based training system, choose the
> Windows Tutorial option from the Help menu in Program Manager.

This is not true for the computer-based training system that comes
with Microsoft Visual Basic. It is a robust training system divided into
sections including: how Visual Basic works, writing event driven programs, working with forms and controls, adding menus, debugging
programs, and using color and graphics. It provides a very good introduction to using Visual Basic.

> **Tip**
>
> To access the Visual Basic computer-based training system, choose the Learn-
> ing Microsoft Visual Basic option from the Help menu within the Visual Basic
> programming environment.

Most of the material covered in the tutorial is the same type of information taught in beginning Visual Basic books. So the question remains if
computer-based training is effective. Personally, I think computer-based
training is effective if done correctly. I just think most people don't know
about these built-in training systems. However, there are probably some
who find the training systems too difficult and intimidating to use.

Reference Material

Many consider the reference section of a manual the most boring element of the documentation. In many cases, the reference section is a
list of every menu command available and a description of what it
does. In other cases, it could be an alphabetical list of Windows API
functions telling the reader what the function does, what parameters it
takes, and what values are returned.

It is important for the reference section to be complete. First, you want to make sure you give the user as much information as possible. Second, if the documentation is left incomplete, your technical support staff will be called upon to answer questions about the holes left in the documentation. You don't want to waste their time with things that you could take care of yourself.

The difference between a manual and a third-party book is that the manual must (should) provide a description of every feature and function in a software package. A third-party book can be written for a certain target audience (for example, a beginner) and can gloss over more difficult parts. The book would give more attention to those topics a beginner may become confused with easily.

> **Note**
>
> Nobody likes third-party books that are blatant rewrites of the documentation. It is a disservice to the reader because these books don't provide any additional information. It is also a disservice to the industry as a whole, because it gives a bad name to books that often can be valuable sources of new information about a subject.

Creating On-Line Documentation

Today, on-line documentation is just about as important as printed documentation. In this world of CD-ROMs that have access to large amounts of information, users expect easy access to an electronic form of printed manuals. Most users expect to search on-line help for a specific keyword and instantly receive information related to that word. Luckily, tools like the Windows help engine (WinHelp) enable you to provide this type of functionality.

Although WinHelp provides many powerful features, it is not the easiest system for which to create document files. It requires documents to adhere to certain guidelines and to be formatted a specific way.

Luckily, there are tools that can help you convert your printed documentation to on-line documentation. Actually, the package I am thinking about provides style sheets you use while writing your documentation. Once you have completed the documentation, you run a set of macros to convert the document files into WinHelp files.

This allows you to provide the exact same type of help on-line as is available in print. Let's take a look at the features that WinHelp provides for the help user.

WinHelp Features

These are some of the WinHelp engine's capabilities that you can add to your own custom help files:

- Text in multiple fonts, sizes, and colors.

- User input through either the mouse or the keyboard.

- Hypertext capabilities that allow the user to locate screens containing related textual information.

- The ability to search for predefined keywords.

- Pop-up definitions that display a pop-up window description of a specified keyword.

- A history list that enables the user to move back through previously browsed material.

- Command buttons to view the previous and next pages. This enables easy navigation through the help system.

- The insertion of 16-color bitmaps or Windows metafiles for inclusion of static graphic images.

The most powerful aspect of WinHelp is its hypertext capability, the use of pop-up definitions, and the insertion of graphic images. Let's examine these a little bit more.

Hyperlinks

Hyperlinks are words that appear by default underlined in green text. Hyperlinks are links (or "jumps") that appear in the help file and enable the user to move to another screen that contains information related to the highlighted text. Hypertext refers to the whole class of documents containing hyperlinks.

When the user moves the mouse cursor over the hypertext word, it turns into a hand cursor. He can then click the left mouse button over the highlighted word, and move to the related text. The keyboard user can select a word by pressing the tab key to select which hyperlink on the screen to jump to and then pressing Enter. Another term used for hyperlinks is cross-references.

Pop-up Definitions

Pop-up definitions are words that appear by default in green with a dotted underline. When the user moves the mouse cursor over the word, it turns into a hand cursor. He or she then can click the left mouse button over the word and a new window that contains the definition of the word appears.

Context Sensitive

Context-sensitive help refers to the ability to query a program for help, and information relating to the task the user is currently working on is displayed. This functionality must be programmed into an application. Adding context-sensitive help requires the coordination of both the programmer (who must display help topics related to the current operation in the program) and writers (who must let the programmer know which topics in a help system relate to specified operations).

WinHelp Authoring Tools

Creating HLP files for the Windows help engine is not the easiest task around, especially if you are in a rush. By using add-in tools you can make the task of creating help files much easier. This section describes some commercial WinHelp authoring tools that are available.

RoboHelp

Blue Sky Software Corporation
7486 La Jolla Blvd., Suite 3
La Jolla, CA 92037
1/800-677-4946 or 619/459-6365
FAX: 619/459-6366

RoboHelp is a Windows help authoring tool that makes creating help files easy. It integrates itself into Microsoft Word for Windows. The product is actually a series of Word for Windows templates, macros, and add-in DLLs that guide the user through the steps of creating help files.

In fact, this tool makes creating help files so easy, you do not have to be a programmer to create help files. RoboHelp generates the necessary Windows help file source code, takes care of running the help compiler, and enables you to test the help system by running WinHelp with your newly created help file.

Doc To Help

> WexTech Systems, Inc.
> 310 Madison Avenue
> Suite 905
> New York, NY 10017

Doc To Help is similar to RoboHelp, but in a way it has more features. It is a series of utilities that works inside Microsoft Word for Windows and makes creating help files easy. It contains predefined Word for Windows templates, in addition to macros that enable you to create professional-looking help files easily.

What is even better about Doc To Help is that you can create manuals and help files at the same time. The same document doubles as the complete documentation for a product, as well as a template which Doc To Help will convert into HLP file format.

Conclusion

This chapter covered the creation of software documentation. You started out learning how to plan the documentation, and continued to gain tips about writing the documentation, updating it, creating tutorials and computer based training programs. The chapter ended with a discussion of the creation of on-line help systems and tools available to facilitate the creation of WinHelp documents.

The following topics were covered in this chapter:

- Before starting to write any documentation you should plan the organization and content of the documentation. One of the easiest ways to plan your documentation is to create an outline for the manual. You should start out with main chapter titles.

- The success of your documentation depends on its usefulness. To make the manual useful, begin with efforts to ensure every element of the documentation is in its place, the right things are explained at the right times, and the needs of the audience (the people who bought your software) receive careful attention.

- Because documentation relies on technical facts, writers must be in constant communication with other people on the team, especially the developers creating the application.

- A tutorial usually includes printed documentation with steps the users follow through, along with data files on disk the user accesses to carry out the tutorial. This is hands-on learning, and many people believe it provides the best way to learn something new, next to having a teacher sit next to you and follow you every step of the way.

- Computer-based training (CBT) consists of tutorials in which the system guides the user through the steps of using an application. With computer-based training systems, there is rarely printed documentation to provide additional help.

- On-line documentation is just about as important as printed documentation. Most users expect to search on-line help for a specific keyword and for related information to be displayed instantly.

Chapter 8

Marketing

A business exists to create and serve valuable goods or services to a customer, selling at a price to result in a profit. This chapter takes a look at the marketing aspect of a business. It is through marketing you get the word about your product out to the public. You find the following topics covered in this chapter:

- You remind yourself who the most important person is at your company.

- You find out what a marketing strategy is and how to develop one for your software product.

- You learn what a unique selling point is and how to create one for your product.

- You find four keys to marketing a product or service.

- You learn why providing a guarantee is important to the success of your company.

By the way, although this chapter specifically focuses on marketing software products, the concepts and principles apply equally well to just about anything you may be selling. After all, the ideas presented in this chapter have been around longer than the software industry itself. They are really universal laws of good business philosophy.

What Is Marketing?

Marketing is the process of continuously telling people about your product. Webster's *New World Dictionary* gives the word an even broader definition, saying that marketing is "all business activity involved in the moving of goods from the producer to the consumer, including selling, advertising, and packaging."

Many people think marketing is running a couple of advertisements in a magazine; however, marketing is much more than just that. It is through marketing you make your product or service known to the public. After all, if the public doesn't know you have a product or service to provide, nobody will be able to take advantage of it.

Marketing is the combination of many other techniques. Advertising, selling, press relationships, partnerships, telemarketing, product endorsements, and product warranties are just some of the components of getting your product known. There are undoubtedly many other techniques. Sometimes the best new product ideas come from a combination of old product ideas.

In the programming community, marketing often gets a bad reputation. For some reason, programmers don't think very highly of the marketing profession in general. I should know; (at heart) I am a programmer, and I have heard all the snide comments. I am sure you have heard the bad lines about "marketing slime" and the "extra" features marketers have added to a product such as the "object oriented this" and the "GUI that" that appear in bold headlines. Well, just like any other profession, there are bad marketing folks, but for the most part this poor attitude of thinking about marketing is out of place and certainly unfortunate.

No matter what type of reputation the people in the marketing department have, marketing is an integral part of any business. Let me repeat that, *marketing is an integral part of any* business. If it weren't for marketing, most companies would not exist.

Before you can reap the benefits of marketing, you must have a great product. Although you can have a poor product and sell it at the beginning of a campaign, if it is bad, sales will slow down dramatically. However, you can have the best product in the world, and without making it known through marketing, you won't sell *any* copies.

> **Note**
>
> I think the poor attitude towards marketing arises when little communication exists between engineers and marketers. Poor communication exists because engineers do not stop to take time to fully explain the product to the people in marketing (probably because they are so busy trying to make the ship date). On the other hand, the marketing people don't ask enough questions about what a product does and what it is for to really make themselves experts on the product.
>
> When I was at Borland, we in technical support were sometimes awestruck by some of the simple—and silly—questions we would receive from people in our company's marketing department. But, to be fair, everybody must learn at some point. At least we were able to set these co-workers straight about how some of the product's features actually worked.

Remember, the marketing techniques presented in this chapter are meant for use on a solid, valuable product. There is nothing you can do to sell a product that doesn't do what it is supposed to. You should make sure the product you are creating fills a need and carries out on its promise.

The Most Important Person at Any Company

You have heard it before, and you will hear it again. The customer is king. This is important. Your customer is the key to your success. You should realize how important your customers are and appreciate them for buying your product. I don't mean the lukewarm, wishy-washy appreciation of customers that most businesses have—and I am not just playing lip service to this concept either.

When I say the customer is king, I am talking about the business's intense desire to provide the best possible service to its customers. Your company should be run and operated as you would expect if you were the customer. After all, if you wouldn't buy something from your own company, who would? Nobody should be more enthusiastic about your product than you and your co-workers.

Many businesses are working to attract new customers; however, they don't realize the huge customer base they already have in their files.

In many respects, your best prospects are your existing customers. The big software companies know this.

There is great potential inherent in any current customer base. The big companies know if they do a mailing to their current customer base, they can expect a certain percentage of those people to purchase the product, no matter what the offer is. This may sound silly, but it is the truth.

> **Note**
>
> I have been using a DOS-based personal information manager (PIM) program for some time. I stopped using it in the past year or so because I had started living in Windows and found it a nuisance to use. Recently, I saw an advertisement for the Windows version of the same PIM. I was ecstatic. Immediately, I called the company and ordered the product. It came with a thirty-day money-back warranty.
>
> Once I received the product, I started using it with a vengeance. Unfortunately, the Windows version of the program was more like a new product instead of an upgrade. Now, I have nothing against new products (in fact I love them), but besides using a different version of data files (I had two years' worth of information stored in the old format) and an interface that was slow and not well-designed (believe me, I see a lot of new programs) the program did not perform well.
>
> So I called the company back up and arranged for a return. They were very nice about the whole procedure; however, they never asked me *why* I was returning the product. I certainly would have taken a couple of moments to explain my dissatisfaction, but they never asked. My question is, "Why didn't they?"
>
> They could have used my feedback to improve the product, but the company chose not to. Obviously they didn't recognize my potential purchasing power over the next few years with new versions of the product.

You should keep an accurate and timely customer list. Updating and reusing your customer list is crucial. These customers bought from you once, and if they had a good experience, they'll buy from you again. Think about it for yourself. If you have a choice of purchasing a product from two companies (assuming the products are equivalent), one company you have bought from before and received excellent products and fantastic service, and the other product from a company you know nothing about, which company would you buy from this time? I think the answer is obvious.

Creating a Marketing Strategy

Your marketing strategy, also referred to as a marketing plan, is a blueprint for how you are going to make your product known to the customer. A marketing strategy is the key to your success or failure in getting the word out about your product.

You need to think about a marketing strategy constantly and continuously check to see if you're on the right track of making your product known. The first step in coming up with a marketing strategy is to think about your product and how you plan to get the word out about it. Working through the details of your plan in advance forces you to be aware of the possible roadblocks and stumbling points that may lie ahead. Furthermore, writing your plans out lets you sort through the many different methods of marketing available and lets you put priority on certain techniques. After all, most companies use a combination of several different marketing techniques. They know each method helps them increase their sales a bit. They also know a combination of the methods helps them drastically increase their sales.

When working on a marketing strategy, you should first understand your organization's mission—the purpose and direction of your company. A marketing strategy outlines what types of marketing methods you will use and how they are carried out.

When working on a marketing strategy, one of the first things you want to do is decide upon a unique selling point for your product.

Unique Selling Point

A unique selling point is the advantage that distinguishes your business and your enterprise from all your competitors. You may have a clear idea about the advantages of your product's features over the competition, but your customers must also be made aware.

You need to find out what is unique about your business, product, or service and then find a way to clearly state that to your customers. Your goal in coming up with a unique selling point is to communicate your product's superiority in a single, well-understood sentence. The unique selling point should reflect something important to your target customers.

> **Note**
>
> Questions to help you decide upon a unique selling point:
>
> - What distinguishes my company from my competitor's company?
> - What distinguishes my product from my competitor's product?
> - Do I render more service than my competitors?
> - Do I give better value then my competitors?
> - Do I provide a better guarantee than my competitors?
> - How does my price compare to my competitor's?
> - What three reasons would my customers give for doing business with me?
> - What results do my customers expect from purchasing my product?
> - Why should my prospective customers choose my product over every other product available?
> - What is the most important thing I can do to make my product unique?
>
> Write the answers to these questions as clearly as possible and use them to help articulate your unique selling point.

You should be able to communicate your unique selling point in sixty seconds or less and you should embed it in your mind so that even if you were awakened in the middle of the night from a deep sleep you could instantly iterate it to a stranger.

It is the advantages of your product you should use as the message you are going to send out to potential customers. You can't build a consistent, effective advertising and selling business if you send out multiple messages about who you are and what your company is about. Many companies try to be everything to everyone; then they can't understand why they don't have any special advantages. The problem is that by being everything to everyone, you can't build any special qualities that differentiate you from competitors. Because you don't come up with any special qualities about your product, it will be undifferentiated—and ignored.

For example, Corel uses the slogan "The Best in Graphics" to portray their advantage of being an excellent graphics manipulation package. Borland's corporate slogan is "The Upsizing Company;" this tells the customer what the company is focusing on.

Once you have come up with a unique selling point, your entire marketing strategy should be based upon it. You can really build your entire business around this as well.

You may even want to modify your unique selling point for each product you are selling. It can help clarify how you are going to sell each product and give you more insight into the advantages of your products.

Another important aspect about your company is its product warranty; we discuss this next.

Product Warranty

Your product's warranty takes the risk of purchasing your product away from the customer and puts it in your company's hands. If you are absolutely sure about your product (and you better be), you should have no concern about taking a risk when a customer is interested in your product. After all, if the product is not useful to the customer, you shouldn't want them to spend money on it.

Typical warranties include:

- "Money-back guarantee!"

- "Thirty-day trial basis!"

- "Satisfaction guaranteed or your money back!"

- "Free trial period. Under no obligation to buy."

- "If this magazine does not live up to your expectations you can cancel at anytime and receive a 100 percent refund of the subscription price."

You have seen all these phrases before; I don't think I am preaching anything new. None of these phrases should be new to you. You have seen them because they work. No matter what you are selling, if you get the product in the hands of the customer without any risk to them and let them decide if it is useful, it will break down the barriers to them trying your product. It tells the customer how you feel about your own product. It also tells the customer you are so confident about their satisfaction and that they will be happy with your product, you want them to make sure for themselves, at no risk to them.

You may be thinking it would be crazy to offer a money-back guarantee with no questions asked. After all, all the customers are going to copy your product, return the disk, and rip you off like crazy. However, it's just not true.

To tell you the truth, this does happen every once in a while. However, by getting the software into the hands of people who would otherwise not have tried it in the first place, you gain new customers. Once they try it (at no risk to them), they might realize that it does indeed fill some need.

You can even extend the warranty further by offering the customer a free "gift" in exchange for trying your product. Even if they return the product, they get to keep the gift. I am sure you have received offers like this before.

If a customer gets something free, even if they return your product, they are much more likely to try it out. Of course, there will always be the small percentage of people who order your product in advance, assuming they are going to return it and then keep the gift. However, I think you will find that, compared to the return on sales you will incur, it is still well worth your time to give away a free gift.

Many companies already provide warranties. However, they don't tell the customer about them. Usually, the warranty is displayed in small type at the bottom of an advertisement. **Put it out in bold type where the customer can see it**. This is especially important for a small, relatively unknown company.

You should use the product warranty as an important part of your marketing plan. Make it very clear to the customer you are taking all the risk and letting them try the product risk free. Making an offer where the customer can't lose will predispose them to try your product. If they try your product and realize they like it, they will then buy it.

The big companies know all about this stuff. Call any of the big software companies and you can be assured that if you are not pleased with the software, you will be able to return it. I think Borland was the first to do this type of product warranty and it resulted in them pioneering it in the software industry and it ultimately resulted in an increased volume of sales for them.

For a customer buying an application from one of the big software companies, the point that you can return software before ninety days have passed has almost become mute. It is almost expected. When working with these big software companies (Microsoft, Borland, Lotus, Novell, IBM, or WordPerfect), people pretty much expect the ability to return the product if they are not happy with it. However, when dealing with a small company, the customer doesn't always expect it.

You can be assured there probably are people who return the product after copying it. But I am sure with the growing complexity of software this is becoming less and less of an issue. Remember, they must return the documentation along with the product, so even if they do return the original product, the copy may be almost useless for them. I like to take the attitude that people usually are honest and responsible, and they won't try to rip you off. Even if they do return the product, you won't necessarily have a lost sale. It could lead to a future loyal customer.

Keys to Marketing Your Product

I know of four keys to marketing your product or service. They include:

- *Specializing* in a specific product category.

- *Differentiating* yourself from competing products.

- *Segmenting* your product to specific customers.

- *Concentrating* your energy in the specific areas you have chosen.

Let's examine each of these concepts in more detail.

Specialization

Unless you have vast resources (like Microsoft, Borland, Novell, or Lotus), you should develop several areas in which your product performs outstandingly. Decide how and why you are going to specialize in a particular area of endeavor. Once you have decided on an area of specialization, become extremely good in that area.

When you specialize, you should find a market small enough to be ignored by the software giants but large enough to support a healthy business. It is pretty obvious that it would be next to impossible to compete in the categories of word processing, spreadsheets, or databases without years of development and huge financial resources to support an incredibly large advertising campaign. Even then, it would be pretty risky. Try to find a market niche.

In fact, it is very smart to create a product which supports another large application. For example, there are companies that thrive on just writing macros for Lotus 1-2-3, or writing font packages for WordPerfect. Recently, a micro-industry has sprung for the add-on custom control market for visual programming tools such as Visual Basic, Paradox for Windows, and Microsoft Access (known as VBX and OCX controls).

When your company specializes in a specific area, you should become as competent in that area as possible. Do everything you can to find out who your competitors are, what they have to offer, and how you can make your product better. You should talk to customers to find out what they want. You should read magazines to find out what they think is important in a product.

If you keep your eyes and minds open you will see new opportunities present themselves continuously.

Differentiation

Decide what you are going to do to be not only different from but better than your competitors. You only have to be better in one specific area to move ahead of the pack. You should decide what this area is, write it down, and then implement it.

Differentiation separates your product from other products of the same type available on the market. You don't want your potential customer thinking your product is exactly the same as your competitor's.

Differentiation can include anything from better documentation and better support to providing more information to your customer. You could give them a video tape or audio tape that teaches them how to use your product. For a programmer's tool or custom control library, you could include the source code.

Promising better support in itself allows you many ways to differentiate your company (and therefore your product) from the competition. I can think of half a dozen right off the top of my head. You can provide on-line support through multiple information services (such as CompuServe, Prodigy, Genie, and the Internet). You can provide 24-hour support or even extended support hours. How about if you provide support on weekends or evenings until 9:00 PM? You can invest in a FaxBack service. You can maintain your own support BBS system. You can even advertise that you have the most helpful or most knowledgeable support personnel. All of these let you differentiate yourself from others.

There are always methods you can use to differentiate your product from others on the market. The rule is to do whatever you can to make sure your product does not become a common commodity.

Segmentation

Look at the marketplace and determine where you can best apply your product's unique selling point to give your company the highest possible return on energy invested. You want to find out exactly who your customers are. This is not always an easy step, but it is important to know who your customers are if you are trying to sell to them.

There are many ways market segments can be broken down. Customer characteristics include knowing your customer by where he lives, his gender, age, or occupation. Business characteristics include the type of business organization that might purchase your software or the company size.

Another method of segmentation is to break down the target user by product factor—that is, concentrating on the product and looking at who would buy this product. Product factors include user characteristics, usage, type of benefits, pricing, and competitors.

For example, user factors would outline the business's market segments by product buyers. Possible user factors for computer buyers might include homeowners, publishing businesses, information processing businesses, or government operations.

When developing a segmentation strategy, decide if you want to restrict yourself to a single market segment or if you want multiple segments. If you decide to employ a single market segment, you must then determine what factor you are going to use to divide your market.

With a multiple segmentation strategy, however, you concentrate on several segments of the market at the same time. When implementing a multiple segmentation strategy, try to make a synergistic relationship between the segment offerings—all the segments should work together. For example, your company might sell a personal information manager and market it to college students (one segment) as well as for home use (another segment). Deciding to whom you are going to sell your product helps your marketing efforts by multiplying them and letting them work together rather than independently.

Concentration

Once you have decided in what area you are going to specialize, how you are going to differentiate yourself, and where in the marketplace you can best apply your strengths, you should concentrate your energy on becoming good at them.

It is a rule that what you concentrate your energies on becomes reality. Therefore, once you have articulated your product's specialty, found out how it is different from other applications, and found your target market, you want to concentrate on these specific aspects of your marketing campaign.

Understanding the Marketing Mix

The textbook definition of the marketing mix (also known as "the four Ps") is a series of four variables marketers consider when deciding on a marketing strategy. The elements in the marketing mix are Product, Price, Promotion, and Place.

Product is what the buyer receives and is usually a service or a tangible item. Price is how much the product or service costs. *Promotion* is what the company does in order to make a product known to its customer. Finally, *place* (or distribution) refers to the location where the product is brought to the customer. For software, this can be mail order, software stores, computer superstores, or retail computer stores like Software Etc. and Radio Shack.

For a business selling software (after all, even Microsoft is small when compared to consumer giants like Proctor and Gamble or Coca Cola), I think there are other, more specific elements of the marketing mix you should use. I like to think of the marketing mix as the combination of methods you use to get your product known to the customer.

Some of the ways you can get your software application known include: advertising, direct-mail campaigns, press releases, publisher relationships, and software bundling, to name just a few. Let's take a close look at what I think are additional elements of the marketing mix.

Advertising

Advertisements are paid messages you make known publicly to prospective customers. Advertising provides a direct line of communication to your current and prospective customers regarding your product or service. You have great control over what you do and don't tell a prospective customer when you run an advertisement.

To get an idea of the power of advertising, trace a typical day in your own life. If you make note of every advertisement you see, you learn we are all continually blasted with messages to buy products and services. I read an article that said once an average American youth reaches the age of twenty-one, that young man or lady has seen beer advertisements or commercials somewhere in the range of 300,000 times. The numbers are absolutely amazing. You can be assured that after having seen 300,000 beer commercials that twenty-one year old might have predispositions to what he is going to drink on his birthday.

By going back to a typical day in the life of the average American, you can see how you are literally bombarded with advertising messages. You see advertisements in the morning paper, you see them on the morning television talk show, as well as on billboards on the way to work and in business newspapers and trade journals at work. If you go out for lunch, you receive many more advertising messages on the trip to and from the restaurant. Then, when you leave work in the evening you get still more billboards, until you make it home and see more commercials during the nightly news.

Don't think the computer industry is immune to this sort of reckless advertising. No matter what trade magazine you look through, you will be literally inundated with advertisements. One of my favorite publications, *PC Magazine*, literally bombards the senses with messages for new monitors, better versions of old applications, and even easier ways to manage finances (these three products were in the first three pages of the magazine's most recent issue).

Advertising's purpose is to accomplish the following:

- Point out a need and create a desire for a product or service

- Announce new products or services

- Draw customers to your business

- Make customers aware of your product or service

- Convince customers your company's product or service is the best available

These are general objectives of creating advertisements. You should also have specific goals developed for each advertisement. Those goals may be to obtain a percentage growth in sales, create more inquiries, or create more store traffic.

You should also try to trace the results of each advertisement you run. This is possible through such techniques as using a different department number for each advertisement you run or by forcing the customer to specify a special number when they place an order. The importance of testing your advertising like this is that you can get a measure of how effective each advertisement is.

A key concept of advertising is that no matter how many responses you get, the advertisement still costs the same. Therefore, if an ad sells 100 products or 1,000 products, the cost to you will still be the same. You want to maximize the number of products you sell for each ad. Because of this, you want to make sure you run advertisements to draw the largest number of responses possible.

Note

You might be saying to yourself this "key concept" of advertising is pretty obvious. However, if it is so obvious, why don't more companies realize this fact? Look through the advertisements in your favorite industry rag, and examine how many companies actually use a system to determine which ad you are responding to.

If you are even more curious, call the company and ask for more information. Some of the smart ones will ask where you saw the ad. However, I bet most of them will not ask where you heard about the product or try to trace the way you found out about it.

When you are keeping tabs of how many people respond to each advertisement you run, you can figure out which is the most effective ad. You can then try to make that ad even more effective. Maybe instead of selling 1,000 products you can change the ad so you double the response rate and sell 2,000 products. Remember, the ad costs the same no matter how many products you sell.

I think by now you can tell almost everybody (unless they live on a remote desert island without running water or electricity) is subject to all kinds of advertising influences. These advertisements must have some sort of effect, because businesses would not continue doing them if they did not receive results.

Let's take a look at several methods of advertising your software product and how they can be used:

- *Magazines.* For the computer industry, advertising through a trade magazine makes the most sense. However, you may find that other (non-industry) magazines can be just as valuable. The key is to test different magazines and find out the results they provide.

- *Newspapers.* An alternative to magazines is advertising in newspapers. The most common choice would be the Wall Street Journal, because of the high number of business people it reaches. However, depending on your target market, the local newspaper might provide you with the exposure your company needs.

- *Coupons.* You can include coupons in an advertisement (but please remember to make them easy to fill out and then send in) or you can create coupons which you get distributors to drop in the box of every order they ship. To give an incentive for the distributor to go to the trouble of inserting your coupon, offer them a percentage of every sale you make as a result of their actions. They will be more motivated to help you. If the idea of splitting the profits disturbs you, ask yourself the question, "Would I be willing to give ten cents away for every dollar somebody makes for me?" Your answer will tell you if coupons might work for you.

- *Billboards.* In Silicon Valley (near where I live), billboards along the highway are a very popular method of advertising both computer hardware and software. They must be effective because they get used. Although this probably only works in an area where large numbers of technical people live, I have seen advertisements for CorelDraw on billboards in San Francisco, California, too.

Also, the technical reviewer of this book told me Microsoft has been advertising on billboards for Word and Excel in rural areas as well as in towns and villages along highways and on the side wall of a local convenience store.

- *Coffee mugs.* Giving away a coffee mug with your product announcement printed on it is a technique used commonly at trade shows. You could even give a coffee mug as a bonus in your software application's box. Then, when the purchaser is in the coffee room and somebody asks him (or her) about the mug, he will be able to rave to associates about the benefits of your software product.

- *Shirts.* I have over a half dozen T-shirts as well as a sweatshirt from Borland with messages about Quattro Pro for Windows, Paradox 4.0, and Borland C++. Although shirts are sometimes the most fun for employees, giving them to customers can be a very effective form of advertising. After all, everybody loves a bonus. If you have a product the customer likes, when somebody asks him about it, he will not be able to stop raving about it. There is no better advertisement than a personal testimony.

- *Buttons.* I am talking about the round type with a pin on the back; people attach them to their shirt or blouse. If you have a catchy logo or a neat phrase, a button is a great way to spread the word. Many computer folks even collect them and pin them to the walls of their office or cubicle.

- *Radio and Television.* This medium is not used much with software, but I believe it will become more prevalent in the future when computers and software become a bigger part of Americans' lives. Intuit has a very powerful "infomercial" that is used to describe the benefits of Quicken. Also, the television advertisement for Apple Computer's PowerBook system has become an instant classic. I have seen it running for over a year, so it must be incredibly effective.

When testing advertising, there are many different variables you can change. I briefly mentioned trying different magazines. Even different trade publications can help. For example, find out the change in response between running the same advertisement in *PC World* versus *PC Magazine*.

Another important change you can make is to change the headline. The headline is the advertisement for the advertisement. It is what entices the reader to continue reading the ad. There are headlines in everything. In a radio commercial, it is the first sentence. In a magazine, the advertisement is usually at the top of the page and is what first catches the eye of the reader.

When creating a headline, try to write one that appeals to a person's self interest. Tell people what your product is going to do for them. Tell them how they will be more productive and more informed by buying your product.

Another type of headline is the curiosity-arousing headline. This headline doesn't necessarily have anything to do with your product but asks readers a provoking question to get them interested. For example:

- "What's wrong with this picture?"

- "Why is this man smiling?"

- "The small fortune you may throw away every day."

You can try adding news value to your headline. Recently, many high-tech advertisements have made references to the "Information Superhighway" popularized by Vice President Al Gore. You also probably have seen many advertisements hyping the benefits of multimedia or some other new technology.

By just changing the headline in your advertisement, you can change the number of responses to the ad. The important thing to remember is to test different advertisements, and then use the most effective ones on a regular basis.

Obviously, classes have been taught and books have been written on advertising. If you find it as interesting as I do, you should definitely follow up by checking out the business section of your local bookstore and pick up a book or two on the topic. Other places to learn more include your local library and being aware of advertising itself. If you study ads you think are particularly effective, they will teach you things you can use in your own business.

Direct-Mail Campaigns

Direct-mail campaigns, a form of direct marketing, are ones seeking an immediate response. That response may be to place an order, ask for more information, return a coupon, make a phone call, or visit a store. As the name implies, this form of marketing uses the medium of mail to provide the customer with information and then asks for the customer to do something.

> **Note**
>
> Shatter the myth that direct-mail campaigns are junk mail. In spite of a bad image, direct-mail campaigns are less intrusive than a phone call or even a television commercial. If the person is not going to buy your product in the first place, all she has to do is throw the ad away.
>
> Junk mail's poor reputation is a result of bad targeting. If you receive direct mail pieces offering a product you have no interest in, that certainly can be considered junk mail. However, if you are a fisherman and receive a catalog of fishing paraphernalia, this is something valuable and you will enjoy reading, even if you don't purchase anything from the catalog.

Actually, direct marketing can take many forms and use many different types of media. Other media types you can use include 900 phone numbers listed in advertisements, telemarketing, and inserts included with other products or in a magazine advertisement. However, we'll concentrate on the use of the mail.

One of the greatest benefits of direct-mail campaigns is that they are easily measurable. That is, you can mail one hundred promotional pieces and easily track how many of those people respond. This is valuable in coming up with new, more effective campaigns.

Creating a direct-mail campaign starts with creating your offer. You must have something the prospective reader can respond to, such as mailing in a card for more information or calling a phone number to order the product. In the offer, you must specify what product you are selling, its warranty, the price, and the action you want the reader of the promotional piece to take. Failure to have a clear offer, or any offer at all, is a common mistake among direct-mail campaigns.

People expect offers when they read promotional pieces. This offer does not necessarily require a customer to buy something. For example, you may decide to offer to send an informational booklet to any prospective customer interested in your product.

An important element of direct-mail campaigns is sending them to the correct people. Your efforts will be useless if you send direct-mail pieces to the wrong individuals. The most common place business finds the names and addresses of prospective customers is through the use of mailing lists.

You can get qualified mailing lists from list brokers (see the yellow pages of your phone book) or you can create your own list from previous purchases of a different product of yours. Precise selection of potential customers is the key to direct-mail campaigns. Lists come in all types and sizes. You should work with the list broker to determine which ones would be best for you.

These lists of names are usually rented. That is, you can only use them once or maybe twice. Expect to pay anywhere from ten cents up to more than a dollar for each name on the list. The difference in price comes from how qualified the list is. For example, there are some people who are more inclined to buy a new product. The addresses for these people cost more than the addresses for those people who are less likely to purchase the product.

It is important to decide how much you want to spend on your direct-mail campaign and then carry out the campaign in a systematic manner. Also, it is wise to test your campaign before you do it on a wide scale. You can test it with just 1,000 direct-mail pieces and find out what type of result it has. If you use similar lists in the future, you can expect the same percentage of results. You can then send to 10,000 or 100,000 individuals and really gear up your selling prospects.

Talking about results, the average response rate for direct mail advertising is 1 per cent. If you get over that, consider yourself having done a good job. If you do less than that, change your offer, or try something different.

So far, the types of marketing we have looked at are those for which you pay. Let's next turn our attention to free publicity.

Press Releases

The written press decides what is good and what is bad and lets people know what they think. As a result, the majority of the industry follows their opinion. One of the most powerful techniques every business should use is free publicity. A good product review or product write-up can help sell a product not just the first time it appears in a magazine, but every time you reprint the review and send it to a prospective customer.

Press releases are a form of free publicity that can infinitely help your company. There is no extra cost to a press release over the time and effort required to attract attention to your business. Only a handful of companies are blessed with a multimillion dollar advertising budget. The companies who don't have incredibly large advertising budgets should take the free publicity they can get and use it to the best of their ability.

There are many reasons for press releases. Perhaps one of the best reasons editorial exposure in a magazine is more valuable than an advertisement in a magazine is that it makes the claims about your product more believable.

Even if your company can afford to and does use paid advertising as a promotional tool, you should still make use of the maximum promotional efforts you can. People have more faith in what they read in the editorial columns of a newspaper or magazine than they have in paid advertising. News is more believable than advertisements.

Note

Press releases that generate product reviews in magazines are good not just for the exposure they provide about your product but also for the exposure they give your company. If you are trying to recruit new talent, that talent is more likely to have heard of your company if it were written up in a magazine. Even if they have not seen write-ups about your product, giving the recruit copies of articles about your company lends credibility to your organization.

In the eyes of potential customers, regular exposure in the media legitimizes your business. If your company name shows up regularly in a positive way, it helps pave the way for when your business goes to the bank for a loan or to work in a partnership with other companies.

After all, if a magazine or newspaper took the time to write about your product and then used valuable space to write a review, there must be something good going on in your company that others don't know about.

I once read that a fast-moving company should have something note-worthy to report to the press every three months. The announcement can be about the release of a new product, an upgraded version of a current product, or a new business alliance with another company. If magazines print your announcement, your company will receive additional publicity.

The book *Do It Yourself Publicity* by David F. Ramacitty contains an entire chapter listing fifty excuses for sending out a news release. Ramacitty even goes so far as to say "virtually any small business can legitimately send out a minimum of six news releases per year." He explains that not all these releases will get you front page coverage; however, even a small write-up in the back section of a magazine or newspaper is better than no publicity at all.

The media finds out about your product or company through the use of a press release. The press release basically gives them the basis for writing a story about your product.

To find out if you have a press release worthy of the media's attention, briefly outline your story idea to several friends, preferably people who are not intimately involved with your company. If their reaction is "Gee whiz, I didn't know that" or words to that effect, you can assume an editor will have the same response, and the story is worthy of a press release.

To find out who to work with at magazines, you should spend time getting to know people at the magazine and developing good relation-ships with them. These relationships can pay off many times over in the future. A simple list of magazines includes:

- *PC Magazine*, the premier PC-related magazine (hence its name). They have the largest circulation of any computer magazine in print.

- *PC World*, another great user's magazine.

- *Windows/Tech Journal*, mainly a technical magazine for Windows programmers.

- *Microsoft Systems Journal*, a definite technical journal for pro-grammers only.

- *Windows/DOS Developers Guide*, another technical journal for programmers only.

- *PC Week*, a "news" magazine, is one of the best sources of new information since it is printed weekly.

- *InfoWorld*, another "news" magazine, comes out weekly and is a great source of new information.

You should seek out other magazines that can be helpful to your product. Obviously, if you are doing Macintosh development the above list doesn't help you much. You know which magazines are hot, and I recommend sending those magazines your information.

Depending on what your product is, you might use one or all of the above magazines. You can find contact information for the magazine (address, CompuServe ID, or electronic-mail address) in each publication. The information usually appears on the page that contains the table of contents, and it is the same page that lists the editors and contributors to the magazine.

So, once you have decided you want to use free publicity to your advantage, and you have decided to which magazines you want to send information, you need to decide what to tell them and how to tell it.

The most likely reason for sending out a press release is the introduction of a new product or an update to a current product. The important principle of writing a press release is to remember why the magazine is going to write about it in the first place. The story must be newsworthy.

If your company is a startup, a great way to make your story newsworthy is to tell your story. Suppose the owner of your company left a promising career at another company, mortgaged his home, then received venture capital funds from a famous VC company. Another story would be if your handwriting recognition technology was developed in what was communist Russia. Make sure the story is interesting.

Another point: remember you don't want your story to sound like it is pushing your product. If you want the magazine to use it, make sure the criteria of newsworthiness is upheld, or some overworked editor will skip over your story for somebody else's story which is actually newsworthy, and makes his job easier.

When putting together your press release, it is a good idea to also put together a media kit. A media kit is a package of information about your company. It can include one or more stories about your organization, photos, information about how the company is organized (sole proprietorship, partnership, or corporation) and anything else important about your company.

Big companies have very impressive media kits, containing professionally written articles, fact sheets, and background information about the company (such things as who founded the company, how many employees it has, and what sort of revenues the company produces). Your media kit does not need to contain everything the big companies have, but it should at least contain several pages of information printed on your letterhead.

The minimum your media kit should have is a description of your product or services, a history of your business, and brief biographical summaries of the founder and key executives. You can put together your own media kit, or you can get a local PR agency to create it for you.

The following are steps to follow when writing your press release:

1. A press release should be printed in letter quality and printed out double-spaced. It should be printed on your company letterhead and look professional.

2. Your company's name and address should be displayed at the very beginning of the press release.

3. Include the name and phone number of a specific person to contact at your company for more information about your product.

4. Write the first paragraph of your press release as an enticement to read the rest. It can be considered the advertisement for the press release.

5. To signify the end of the press release, use three pound signs, "# # #."

Inside the text of the press release, remember to answer who the press release is about, what your press release is announcing, when your product will be available, where it can be obtained (directly from the company, at software stores, and so on) why the news release is important and how much it will cost.

These are the five Ws you learned about in high school English class—who, what, when, where, and why. Another aspect not covered by these five Ws is "how," but adding it ensures all the information is obtained. For your press release to be printed, it is important to make sure the magazines are aware of all the vital facts. Listing 8.1 gives you a sample press release.

Listing 8.1 Sample Press Release.

FROM: Bob Brown, Public Relations Manager

Super Software Company

1234 1st Street

Anytown, California 12345

Phone: 123/456-7890 x 765

Fax: 987/654-3210

FOR IMMEDIATE RELEASE

NEW SOFTWARE PRODUCT TEACHES PEOPLE HOW TO SPEAK

On Tuesday, April 10, 19xx, Super Software Company, headquartered in Anytown, California, introduces a new type of database product, called SpeakEasy, that uses the advanced features of multimedia technology to actually teach people how to speak.

Jack Jones, president of Super Software, first discovered the secrets of teaching people how to speak while on a trip to Jamaica. The locals brought to his attention the age old principles they have kept in their own community.

By using multimedia software found in the Microsoft Windows operating environment, Mr. Jones was able to bring this ancient Jamaican learning method to the high-tech desktops of information professionals in businesses around America.

The speech training system requires a PC based system running a 486 microprocessor with Microsoft Windows for Workgroups. The product costs $999 and is available direct by calling 555/123-4567.

# # #

Make sure there are no typographical errors in your press release. After all, if there are errors in your release, an editor will think "if they don't care enough to spell it right, they probably don't care enough to have us use it." Also, make sure each press release looks good and is professionally duplicated. Make it easy to read and make sure it isn't smudged, has pale impressions, or is crooked on the page. With a laser printer, this should be no problem. Also, print your press release on plain white paper with black ink. Don't try to be fancy and use colored paper or special inks; these are usually harder to read, and editors are already overworked as it is.

Like advertising, the area of public relations is a field in and of itself. If you want to create publicity for your company, I highly recommend Ramacitty's book as a good introduction.

Publisher Relations

Most big companies have a special group of people who work with outside publishers and authors. The purpose is to provide support in the form of early (beta) releases of products, information about products, and anything else they may need.

I know most small businesses can't expect to have a book written about their product, but this is a good thing to keep in the back of your mind in case your company grows larger.

It is vitally important to provide as much information to authors and publishers as you can. Having third party books, magazines, and products available that support your product can only help you. The existence of these other products gives your application much more credibility, because the end user can see there is a demand for more information on the subject than just what you provide.

In fact, Microsoft realized back in 1985 how important the aspect of third party books is. In addition to forming a department of people who work with book publishers and authors to support their products, they created their own publishing arm (Microsoft Press, wholly owned by Microsoft) that only publishes books about Microsoft products. Pretty smart idea, don't you think?

Borland knows the power of having a line of books supporting their products. Although they don't have their own publishing arm, they formed a partnership with another publisher to print books that contain the Borland name and logo on the front, as well as a foreword written by Phillippe Kahn, Borland's CEO.

This phenomenon is not unique. I have seen partnerships of Novell, WordPerfect, and Symantec with book publishers to have books that contain the company's "official seal of approval" printed. It is a powerful way of adding credibility to a product.

Software Bundling

Software bundling is a partnership between your software company and a hardware company. The idea is to pre-install your software on the computers the hardware company is selling. Microsoft is famous for this. They have done a very good job of getting their software pre-installed on computers. How many computers have you looked at lately that don't come bundled with DOS and Windows?

> **Note**
>
> It has been said that before Windows became wildly popular, Microsoft literally gave copies of it away to hardware vendors for bundling in the hopes end-users would select it as their operating environment of choice.
>
> Microsoft was betting that once people started using Windows, they would soon start purchasing applications that would run under the environment. I think you will agree the bet paid off. Microsoft now reaps much of their profit through the sale of application software which runs (coincidentally enough) under Windows.

CD-ROM drive makers have done this for some time. It has really helped make CD-ROMs gain acceptance. The idea is that when you buy the drive, you also get five or six applications on CD-ROM. This helps sell applications for the software companies as well as helping sell CD-ROM drives.

Bundling is powerful, because you get a lot of copies of your software available to end users when they first buy their computer. If they like your software, it is likely they will purchase other products from you.

Bundling looks good for the hardware companies, too. They pay you a small fraction of the list price for your software, but they buy a lot of copies. They provide this to the customers who would have to pay much more for the product if they purchased it separately.

Software bundling can become even more lucrative if you allow the customer to upgrade the software at a "reduced price." This provides additional sales for you in the future, and as I mentioned, if the customer is happy with the product, it becomes an even easier sale for the software company.

Partnerships

Another type of software bundling occurs when two companies with complementary products sell their products together. Before the companies merged, Intuit and Chipsoft sold Quicken and TurboTax together in one package. These two software applications—finances and tax preparation—complement each other very nicely and were perfect matches to sell together in one box.

Borland and WordPerfect sold the Borland Suite, a combination of Quattro Pro, Paradox, and WordPerfect. These three products packaged together provided a tremendous benefit to the customer and also allowed the two companies to produce a package that offered many more features.

It is important to realize the marketplace is expecting applications that work together. The customer doesn't want several applications bundled together that don't also work together. The programs should share data and work together in an associated matter.

The 800 Order Line

An 800 order line makes doing business with your company easy, appealing, desirable, and even fun. When somebody calls your telephone number it means he is interested in your product. Your company should be ready to help the customer however it can, if that includes giving him more information about your product or taking his order for him.

It is amazing how many times I have called a company for more information about a product, and then waited weeks to receive information about that product. By the time I received the information, I either found another product or I no longer needed the product. Timing is important.

Remember that when somebody asks for information about your product, they are already predisposed to buying your product. I think you should try to get their information as soon as possible.

The person answering the phone at your business makes the first impression to a customer about what it is like dealing with your company. Many companies pay high salaries to software engineers, but when it comes to the person who answers the phone, they find a temporary worker, or hire somebody at minimum wage and give them no training as to how they should act. This is ludicrous.

Because the people answering the telephone make a big impression, your company should at least train them to know where callers should be directed for information. They also should be polite, courteous, and helpful.

The people answering an order line should be especially helpful. Obviously, taking orders is a repetitive, sometimes boring job. However, your company would benefit by making sure these people are trained and motivated so they will treat the customer right.

Selling Razor Blades

I don't know what the marketing profession calls this, but the idea was first capitalized on by Gillette. The way it works is that you give away the razor (or sell it at price to cover your expenses) and then sell the razor blades. Since the razor blades are consumable, you can make a better return and sell a greater number of them.

In the software industry, Intuit does this very effectively with its Quicken personal finance application. The software itself sells for about fifty dollars. At this price, the company is just covering their expenses. They really make money by selling special checks that fit in your printer and are guaranteed to work with their software. Notice the similarities between finance software and checks versus razors and razor blades. Both razor blades and checks are consumable. They are used up and people need more of them. The other thing is that once you start using them, it is hard to go without them.

If you can find this same sort of relationship between two products you sell, you should use it to your advantage. You are providing a valuable service to your customer, and at the same time making a healthy profit for yourself.

Software Upgrades

As you know, upgrades are an invention of the software industry. Companies are aware of the gold mine they have available to them in the form of customers who will always upgrade to the newest version of a product, no matter how many changes are made and how much it costs.

The big companies even have plans for how many new releases and upgrades they are going to make available for their products. Microsoft has plans for the next five years for their upgrade path and for what features are going to be added to their products.

The concept of a software upgrade should not be undervalued. However, you don't want to take advantage of the customer. Selling an upgrade that has no added value is a way to turn off customers who upgrade and also a way to waste your resources. You should always make sure a new upgrade has some specific advantage and then point out these advantages to the customer in your upgrade literature.

Competitive Upgrade Policies

Borland took a lot of business away from Lotus when they first sold Quattro Pro for DOS and offered the "competitive upgrade offer." Borland let you have Quattro Pro at a special price not only if you had an old version of Quattro, but also if you had an old version of 1-2-3 (as well as several other competing spreadsheets).

It was an incredibly smart marketing move for Borland. The most important reason for this is that many of the new customers they obtained found out how much they loved the product, and kept on upgrading their software with every new release. This provided much more additional revenue, because the company was able to capitalize on selling upgrades as well as attracting new customers for the product.

Planning for the Product Ship Date

We have taken a pretty good look at ways you can market your software product. One of the things you should think about while you are developing your marketing strategy is planning for the product ship release.

Planning for product ships concerns the logistics of getting your product into the customers' hands. It includes the details of getting disks duplicated, documentation printed, packaging developed, and shrink wrap applied.

Depending on your company's size, you may or may not want to do these functions yourself. Even big companies like Borland outsource these activities to firms that specialize in them. This takes a big burden away from your company and allows it to focus on what you want to do—developing software, rather than copying disks, creating disk labels, and putting together packages.

You can find companies that provide these services by looking in the phone book or by contacting associates who have worked with companies that provide these services. Either way, it is best to get a recommendation from somebody else. This provides you with the level of service the company will provide.

Conclusion

This chapter covered marketing software products. It started by describing how to create a unique selling point. It then described how to use this unique selling point as the basis for your entire marketing campaign.

In particular, the following topics were covered:

- Marketing is the process of continuously telling people about your product.

- Your marketing strategy, also referred to as a marketing plan, is a blueprint for how you are going to make your product known to the customer.

- The customer is king. A business should have an intense desire to provide the best possible service to their customers. Your company should be run and operated as you would expect it to be run if you were the customer.

- A unique selling point is that distinct, appealing idea that sets your business apart from every one of your competitors. Your goal in coming up with a unique selling point is to communicate your product's superiority in a single, well-understood sentence.

- Your marketing strategy, also referred to as a marketing plan, is a blueprint for how you are going to make your product known to the customer.

- Four keys to marketing a product or service include specializing in a specific product category, differentiating yourself from competing products, segmenting your product to specific customers, and concentrating your energy in your chosen areas.

Chapter 9

Technical Support

This chapter takes a good look at working in technical support. You learn what technical support is about, how to provide great support, and how to make the customers feel good about the service they get. You also learn about methods you can use to improve a technical support program.

In particular, the following topics are covered:

- What the purpose of technical support really is.

- How the economies of the computer industry demand that technical support groups use every piece of technology available to them.

- How to set and meet customers' expectations. Why it is important to do follow up on customers' expectations.

- Some methods to use when talking with customers.

- Techniques you can use to troubleshoot problems for customers.

- How to make the job of technical support easier by having customers prepared.

- How to close a call.

- Simple methods a technician can use to improve his or her own technical skills.

- Alternate methods (other than telephone calls) you can use to provide support for your product.

- How to keep technical support staff motivated, and ways to prevent job burnout.

Purpose of Technical Support

The sole purpose of technical support is to provide service, advice, and assistance to a customer in the use of a software product. This assistance can be on any level, all the way from helping a customer install an application that won't install correctly, to providing theoretical assistance on the use of the product.

This definition of technical support may seem obvious; however, many times technical support turns into a baby-sitting program for users who don't bother to read manuals, users who would rather not bother to research a problem for themselves, or people who don't give a darn and are calling because somebody else (their boss) told them to. Before a company can provide technical support, it must decide what level of support it can afford to provide. Providing even minimal technical support is expensive.

Deciding on the level of technical support to provide for your product can be challenging. If you provide too much support, you may end up with too many people working in support (that is, people sitting around doing nothing, waiting for phone calls). If you don't provide enough support, a company can get a poor reputation.

The Economies of Technical Support

Several years ago, when a software product sold for $495.00, consumers felt technical support was part of what they were buying. Today, when a consumer buys that same product at one tenth the previous cost, it becomes increasingly difficult for the company to provide the same level of support as when the product sold for a higher price. Unfortunately, the user still feels technical support is something they paid for and deserves.

As you probably know, many companies, including Microsoft, Borland, and Lotus, are moving to paid support programs. These come in the form of paid support numbers (900 numbers), paid-in-advance programs, and corporate support programs costing the customer thousands of dollars. As software companies have come to find, the cost of support can be the single most expensive cost center for a product.

At Borland, management calculated that every five minute phone call a support engineer took cost the company $27. That price includes the technician's salary, building rent, lighting, computer equipment, and every item required to provide support.

Let's look at these numbers closely. When a product sells for $49 (such as Quattro Pro for Windows), and the materials to produce the software (manuals and disk) cost $5, a single call which lasts eleven minutes (the average length of most support calls) ends up losing the company money. Most companies are not in the business to lose money.

Obviously, not everybody calls technical support. If they did, the companies certainly would be out of business. I suppose the 80/20 rule applies here. This rule, applied to technical support says that only 20 percent of the customers will call with complaints; however, the support staff will spend 80 percent of their time with these customers.

Note

The 80/20 rule says that eighty percent of a resource will be spent on twenty percent of another resource.

For example, eighty percent of a salesperson's time will be spent on twenty percent of her customers.

It also says that eighty percent of a company's business will come from twenty percent of its customers.

Another example is that you wear only twenty percent of your available clothing eighty percent of the time.

Most People Don't Need Technical Support

The great number of support calls is especially difficult for a company when the customer calling is somebody who does not bother to check the README file for additional information. It gets even more challenging when the customer assumes that because the company has a technical support line, these technicians will teach the user how to use a product (what a spreadsheet is for, how to program in C, or how he can use a database to keep track of his stamp collecting hobby). Certainly the role of technical support cannot be that of teaching a user how to use a product. After all, you don't get free driving lessons when you buy a car.

As a result, creating a technical support department requires using every available means of cutting costs and making information available to the customer. In fact, it is becoming more common to actually turn technical support from a profit loss center into a profit earning department (or at least break even) through the use of paid support programs.

Meeting Expectations

The most important aspect of technical support is meeting customer expectations. Meeting customer expectations means telling the customer what you are going to do for them and then turning around and actually doing what you said you were going to do. What a novel approach.

Basically, meeting customer expectations means telling the customer what you can do for them and following through on that promise.

For example, if you are going to mail a customer an update disk, and you know it will take a minimum of five days to arrive, tell the customer it will take at least this long. Then, when he or she is waiting for the package to arrive, they won't be wondering when it will appear, how much longer it will take, and even if they will ever receive the package in the first place. You have met their expectations.

One time, a colleague of mine had promised to send the newest version of a product to the customer. My friend had originally been told the new version would be ready in several days. Well, the days came and went. He had originally told the customer the disks should arrive in two weeks.

After two weeks' time, he called the customer and told him it was still not available. My friend made it clear he was still planning to send the disks out when they were available. It turns out, this process went on for about eight weeks, where every two weeks my friend would call the customer and tell him the same story.

In the end, the customer wrote a flattering letter to the manager in charge of support (my friend's boss's boss) and praised everything my friend had done. Can you believe that? It took four times longer to receive the package than originally promised. This story shows you that even if there is a major delay or problem, and the support person handles the issue in a professional manner, it still can satisfy the customer.

Obviously this does not apply to every customer. Some customers don't ever want to be happy and there certainly will be times when nothing you can do makes a customer happy. At these times, probably the best thing is to do whatever you promised you would, and then pass them on to a supervisor. Sometimes all a customer wants is to feel like someone is listening to their ideas. It is then your duty to pass the customer on to a supervisor. That is what the supervisor is there for. They know that as well as you do.

An important element of meeting customers' expectations is telling them just how long it will take to do something. An example is putting a customer on hold. Just before you put the call on hold, first ask them if it is all right. They are always going to say yes. If they say no, tell them you are doing whatever you can to help them, and if they won't cooperate, there is nothing else you can do.

Next, tell the customer what you are going to do and how long you expect it to take. For example, "I would like to research this printing issue further. I think it will take about five minutes. Is it OK if I put your *call* on hold?" Notice the wording. You never want to put a *customer* on hold, instead you want to put their *call* on hold. This may sound like a minor difference, but in truth it is much nicer to put a call on hold (an intangible, impersonal object), rather than putting the customer (the person who gave your company money) on hold.

> **Note**
>
> When I first began working in support and was answering calls for Borland's Quattro Pro spreadsheet, I once received a call from a woman who started the conversation "I am using Quattro Pro because a client demands it. I hate the program, and I don't want to use it at all."
>
> Do you think, that when the conversation was initiated this way, it made me feel very good? Obviously not. From experience I can tell you the technician is more likely to help a customer when he starts a conversation with something like "I love your product; I think it is great. I am probably just a dummy, but I don't know how to blah blah blah. Could you please help me?" In fact, I would bend over backwards to do whatever I could to help a customer who spoke to me like this.
>
> On the other hand, criticizing the product does not help the customer's point. After I talked to this woman for an hour and a half, she was still not pleased. She was trying to do something Quattro Pro could not do. She expected me to provide patches to make the product do what she wanted. In the end I passed her to my manager who told her the exact same thing I had said.
>
> How would you have handled this call?

Meeting customers' expectations comes down to communicating to them what you are going to do, how long it is going to take to do it, and why you are going to do the specified action. Even if you plan to take a specified action for a customer, and don't tell her, the customer won't be satisfied. A customer who does not know what you are going to do, and why you are going to do it thinks you (and therefore the company) don't care.

Talking with Customers

Anybody working in technical support must understand they are the company's representative. To many customers, the technical support representative *is* the company. Therefore, it is imperative for the technician to act properly, respond appropriately, and to interact with the customer in a professional manner.

A technician can act properly by imagining the customer is actually there with him—one on one, face to face. It may sound silly, but if you smile while talking on the phone, it comes through on the other end of the line in the sound of your voice. I knew friends who actually had small mirrors in their cubicles for this reason. They even had small signs that said "Smile." They weren't trying to be cute by doing this. They knew the value of smiling. You might want to remember the old cliché about how it takes less muscles in your face to smile than it does to frown.

You can respond appropriately to a customer by listening to what the customer has to say. This is much easier said then done, especially when the customer is asking the same question you have already answered a hundred times this week, and you know the answer immediately, before the customer is even done asking the question.

You should at least give the impression you are listening to the customer by letting them finish what they are saying before you start speaking. You can also respond by changing the tone of your voice and by acknowledging what the customer is saying.

Acting in a professional manner includes all the common courtesies any businessperson would use when talking on the phone. Don't talk when you are eating. Don't chew gum. Say "yes" rather than "yeah" and speak clearly.

When talking to customers, always refer to documentation by section or chapter rather than by page number. This is because, if there have been several versions of the manual, the page numbers could be different. If the customer forces a page number out of you, it is best to say "around page 452." You can then lead him to the exact location by referring to headings and titles.

Another point. It is truly amazing. Many people hear a technician typing on a keyboard and it immediately makes them feel uneasy; they don't think the technician is listening to them. Try to make sure that unless you are entering their name into a database (and they know you are), they can't hear you typing.

These are all simple tips. In fact, you may be wondering why you are reading about them in a book. However, in practice these techniques are much easier to give lip service to than to actually carry out. Although they sound easy, it can be frustrating when you have a bossy, arrogant jerk on the other end of the line.

Just try to smile and keep your cool. Then on top of that, acknowledge the customer's feelings. When they say you are supporting a crummy product, thank them, in a friendly voice, for calling. You can tell I have had some experience in this area before. That is why many of us need to be reminded continually about phone etiquette.

Troubleshooting

Troubleshooting is the process of finding out what is causing a problem or learning what a customer is doing. A customer often will tell you what the problem is. However, sometimes what they think the problem is has nothing to do with what they are doing. It is up to the technician to find out what the real problem is. It is not enough to lead them on a trail that won't help them solve their problem's cause—especially since most often they will call back and need more assistance. If at all possible always do as much as you can for them when you have them on the phone.

I would say the most important element of troubleshooting is asking questions. By asking intelligent questions, you can find the answer to almost any problem. You might find an answer you don't want to hear, but at least you will find an answer.

Note
Summary of the elements of technical support:
Ask questions.
Listen to what the customer has to say.
Act in a professional manner.
Don't type while you are listening to the customer.
Smile and keep your cool.

You need to ask very specific questions. Keep in mind the many examples of communication errors. The program that says "Press Any Key to Continue" and people call, asking where the "Any" key is on their keyboard. There is also the case of a support representative asking the user to close the door (referring to the disk drive door), and having the customer jump up and actually close the door to his office. There are many examples of miscommunication, and it is very important for the technician to verbalize exactly what they are trying to say. On the other hand, pampering an experienced user can infuriate them all the same.

Sometimes people don't even know the problem they are having. They might have difficulty describing what is happening. If they are just learning to program, they may not know what a GP fault is. This is especially true for those people just getting started with the software.

If a customer does not know what you are talking about, you should try to describe it to him in clear terms. However, if the customer does understand what you are talking about, you should try to meet him at his level. If the customer is talking about implementing a DDE server, you obviously should not describe what the "Any" key is. He will feel you are talking down to him, and could react in a negative manner.

On the other hand, if the customer is at the level where he does not know where the "Any" key is, make sure you don't talk down to him. He probably already feels like a dummy, and the last thing he needs is somebody in support to treat him like one. This is a vital step towards good customer relations.

Once a technician has found out what is causing a problem, he must move on to find a solution to the problem. If you know what the problem is, it is not as difficult to find the solution to the problem. It is easier for a support technician to ask assistance from a colleague when he has a question, than it is if he has to describe an entire situation.

Finding the solution can include checking the product documentation, checking a support database, or even checking for technical documents that have been written to help the customer.

What Is a Problem?

At Borland, we were always taught never to refer to a problem as a problem. That is, we were supposed to refer to a customer's questions as "issues," "situations," or "challenges." There was no such thing as a problem. The reason for this is that problems are just that—a problem. In most people's minds *problems* represent a big, difficult, hard-to-solve task. However, when referred to as an *issue*, it removes the customer's mental roadblock of being a problem and makes it easier to deal with.

It is surprising, but by removing the mental roadblock of calling a problem an issue, we came much closer to solving it. In some instances, customers preferred calling them problems; however, by controlling our own language, we were able to keep them as issues.

You might say there really are problems that are more then just "issues." In fact, we would probably call them software bugs. This brings me to another topic. We were not supposed to refer to bugs as bugs. Instead, they were called technical limitations. The reason for this was that bugs are bad. Technical limitations are not any fault of the company.

Helping Yourself

There are definite ways to make providing technical support easier. It all starts out by telling the customers what they should already know before calling. When you list a technical support telephone number, ensure that you tell the customer to have pertinent information ready at the time of the call. This might include a serial number, version number, AUTOEXEC.BAT and CONFIG.SYS file listings, along with pertinent information about special requirements of the software.

> **Note**
>
> Many times, I would talk to somebody who wanted to know the answer to some type of technical question. I would ask him for some information about his computer system and he would not know the answer. Worse yet, he was often a computer hobbyist, rather than a professional, and did not even use the computer at work—where he was calling from!
>
> Since it was his personal computer, he did not have access to the computer (or often *any* computer) at the time of the call. So even if I tried to ask for some information to solve his problem, he couldn't provide any.
>
> There is absolutely no way in the world I could provide technical support to somebody who is not even in front of his computer. I can give him vague ideas, but it is extremely difficult to get him going.
>
> The best way to handle this situation was to just tell the customer the truth, that it is very difficult to track down the problem if he is not in front of the computer. I would give him the first things I would try so at least he would have something to work with when he got home.

Another way to take the load off the technical support staff is to have a senior technician record answers to common questions. Provide a method for the customer to listen to these common questions before she talks to a real person. This might sound impersonal, but a customer would rather listen to a recording of the answers to questions than wait on hold.

On the side of support personnel, if a customer can listen to a recording that answers repetitive questions, it beats having a person talk to her and go over the same boring solution with her one more time.

Obviously, you must choose the recorded messages appropriately. You want to keep track of the common questions, and provide answers to those questions.

Closing a Call

Having satisfied customers is great. However, even if somebody is happy with your support and your company's product, you can't talk to him all day. In fact, you want to minimize the length of each call as much as possible.

Some people you talk to are so excited with what they are doing that they want to tell you about how they are using your software, what they are using it for, and how they wrote this incredible program to keep track of their farm animals.

> **Note**
>
> No kidding. I once talked to a man who used Quattro 1.0 (the predecessor to Quattro Pro) to keep track of the cows on his farm. He was proud of the fact, and to tell you the truth, I was pretty impressed that this guy working in a low-tech field was using high-tech methods to manage his business.

This is when you need to learn how to close a phone call. Many times asking them a simple question such as "Is there anything else I can help you with?" will make him realize you have answered all his questions. However, this one can sometimes backfire because although you had fully answered his original question, he will think of some new questions to ask you.

Therefore, you can use something to the effect of "Well, I guess that answers all your questions." Another one presupposes you have answered his questions and moves to close the call with "Thanks for calling." If she has made some comments (good or bad) about the program, you can tell her you will make sure her comments are passed on to the developers. You (obviously) want to make sure the developers are notified about what the customer had to say.

Preparing for Technical Support

The term "Knowledge is Power" applies even more when referring to technical support. During the time you answer phone calls, you will be called upon to answer some of the most bizarre questions thinkable.

You might wonder to yourself why in the world anybody would want to do something a specific way, but just remember they are the customers. If they want to do something a specific way, you should do your best to try to help them use the software. As an alternative, if you know what they are trying to accomplish, you can point them to the most efficient method of doing what they want, or you can point them to available add-ons that will help them.

This is also a tremendous source for new ideas and improvements to the software too. After all, rather than insisting on doing things an "approved" way, by offering options or alternatives your product may satisfy a broader market.

One of the best ways to help the customer is to keep a piece of paper next to your phone. When you are answering questions, and you come across one which you are not 100 percent sure of the answer to, write it down. Then, in your time off the phones, you can research the problem. Many times by talking to a senior advisor (somebody who has been working in support for over 18 months) you will find the answer immediately. Other times, you might need to look something up in the manuals or check a third-party book for the answer.

If different parts of the company work together, Technical Support should talk to the Documentation department to ensure software documentation is updated and easier to understand. Even better, if there are operations customers find truly difficult, Technical Support can pass this feedback on to the Developers, who can use it to improve the software.

Having the Information Ready

Technical support can be much more than just talking to somebody on the phone. Great technical support staffs provide alternate methods for customers to help themselves. Most often taking telephone calls is the most common aspect of technical support. Increasingly there are other, more effective ways of helping customers.

The first obvious choice is through U.S. mail, or an overnight package carrier (FedEx, Airborne Express, and so on). This method is probably the most inefficient method of providing support. First, these carriers are the most expensive method of providing information, and second because they take a lot of the technician's time to prepare.

The most obvious choice is through a fax. This entails having a facsimile machine, having somebody watch for the faxes, read them, write a response, and fax them back. Commonly you respond to a customer in the same way they originally communicated with you.

Today, with talk of the information superhighway, electronic services such as CompuServe, BIX, Genie, and the Internet are extremely popular methods of providing support. The reasons are obvious. It is much easier to respond to electronic messages, and the speed at which the user gets a reply is much faster than waiting for paper mail.

Another important element of the information superhighway is on-line support. A common example is a CompuServe forum. Both Borland and Microsoft have several forums where users can post messages, download related software (or even program updates), and just share information.

A FaxBack service (a semi-electronic form of communication) can be incredibly useful. You have a toll-free phone number to provide technical documents that are faxed to the customer at no charge. These documents have been written by technicians and they each target a specific problem. They can be anywhere from one to ten pages long (or however long you are willing to have), and they provide specific answers to common questions. Customers call and enter the technical information document number with the touch tone pads on their fax machine. The information is then faxed back to the customer immediately.

The idea is, that by providing this free service, the technicians can be freed up to help other customers, or to write new technical information documents.

Call Management

Borland had some pretty advanced methods of managing their calls. Of course, when you receive more phone calls than the rest of the city combined, it is easier to work with the phone company to find alternate means of providing phone numbers!

With the huge number of phone calls we received, Borland also invested heavily in state-of-the-art phone systems. We knew instantly how many calls we had answered in a day, the average length of the calls, how many outgoing phone calls we had placed in the day, and how many calls we had answered by the hour.

This information is valuable not only to managers, but also to the technician. Assuming you want to maximize the time you spend on the phones, you want to answer as many phone calls as possible. By learning methods to speed up call taking, you can improve the number of calls you answer in a day, and therefore increase the number of calls in a day.

Note

In an eight hour day, we were expected to answer phones for five hours, and use the remaining three hours to answer faxes and letters, and research ongoing problems. Management wanted us to answer seven calls per hour, so this translated to a minimum of 35 calls per day. In fact, we were expected to be answering this number of calls once our training was over.

There was lots of pride involved with the number of calls we answered in a day. The record was some guy who answered 167 calls in one day. I think my best was 87.

Getting Feedback

One of the very best ways to get feedback is to record your calls and listen to them. Imagine you are the customer on the other end of the line.

Listening to your own phone calls can be one of the most valuable experiences available. By listening to them after the call has happened, you can gain a lot of insight and knowledge about how to respond to customers. Remember, it is illegal to tape a phone conversation unless you first get permission of the other party. Many software companies have a recording in which they say calls may be recorded.

If you really want to improve your phone calls, listen in on phone calls by other technicians. If at all possible, listen to phone calls by the senior advisor. It is very interesting to hear the different ways people respond to the same question.

Paid Support Programs

Increasingly, technical support programs are turning from cost centers into profit centers. The most obvious result of this is the emergence of pay by call (900 lines) phone numbers, which automatically bill the caller by the length of the call.

However, there are other paid support programs a company can use. If you have a big customer who buys many copies of a product, you can give him his own support telephone number. If you have several large customers, you can share a single number among several customers. They will feel better because they are getting premium support, and you are happy because they have bought many copies of your product.

As for charging for a service like this, you can either make it a bonus when the customer buys so many copies, or you can charge a premium price for the service. You can also sell contracts for unlimited support for a certain length of time—say 30, 90, or 120 days. Even better, you could create contracts for six months up to a year or more.

As you can see, there are many ways to be creative when it comes to paid technical support programs.

Productivity Management

Because of the costs involved with technical support, the company you are working for will probably want to minimize the time you spend on each call. A good way to do this is to keep a sheet of paper on your desk on which you can write down the length of the call, and what it was about. If you notice a certain type of call taking a long time, find a way to describe the problem quickly. Or, even better, write a document about the issue that you can fax or mail to customers.

Keeping Track of Your Calls

The best way for you, as a support technician, to stay on top of things is to keep track of your calls. This can be done in several ways, but this is the easiest method: Every time a question comes along that can't be answered, write it down on a piece of paper. Then, in your time off the phones, go research the answer to the question. Find out the answer and write it down. Next time, when that question comes up, you will probably remember the answer. Even if you don't remember the answer, you can check your notes.

After a short while, you won't need your notes anymore. In fact, others will come to you for answers. You will be the new guru.

Keeping Tech Support Motivated

I know some people will argue with me, but in some ways technical support is one of the most difficult jobs anybody can have. Not only are you being bombarded with questions all day long, of which you might get some you have no idea how to answer but, usually you only deal with people who are having problems and are often in an abusive state of mind. These people are mad, frustrated, and upset. Often, it is the technician who takes the abuse of an angry customer, even if the problem is a bug or manual misprint that was no fault of technical support.

On the other hand, support can be one of the most rewarding jobs available. Rarely do other people at a software company get to work directly with customers. Technicians are on the front line (so to speak) and they know exactly how the customer feels, what features they like and dislike in a product.

Furthermore, no other department provides such opportunity for learning a product. Nowhere else will you be answering questions all day long about your product, from such a variety of users. In many companies, those individuals responsible for technical support have an overall knowledge about a product greater than anybody else in the company. They probably know even more than the developers. This is because the developers know about their area of expertise (that is, the part of the product they develop). Otherwise, they don't know much about the rest of the product.

With all the stress put on technical support individuals, it can sometimes be difficult to keep them motivated. Job burnout is a common factor in technical support. Therefore, as a technical support department grows, it is important to continually invent ways to reward the senior members of a team, and keep them on board.

The obvious answer is to raise their salary. This can certainly help, but you must keep in mind that there are other methods to use as well. As technicians get to know a product, promote those persons to senior technicians. In this role, they provide more help to other junior technicians. They also focus themselves on writing technical information documents which can be transmitted to customers. They also should involve themselves with training programs and listening in to support calls and critiquing them.

Although there are always surprises with new phone calls, after about a year of answering calls, there are not many you have not heard. The difficult time comes when a new product is announced, and a flood of new phone calls arrive. It is at these times when the senior technician can be the most helpful, by being available for other technicians, and pitching in on the phones.

To me, letters from satisfied customers are some of the most prized possessions. Most people would agree that helping somebody out and then receiving a letter from them about how great he is can be very rewarding. If you take these letters (or copies of them) and make a bulletin board, it keeps technicians motivated. It is a very effective way to keep technicians focused.

The Future of Technical Support

As software becomes even more complex, the role of technical support will become even more important. The catch-22 is the increasingly less-expensive cost of software and the exponential cost of hiring well-trained individuals to staff support lines.

To me, the solution is to use technology to provide support. Some of the methods described earlier include FaxBack services and electronic support through CompuServe or a BBS. Although these may seem like a cold way to offer support, it seems to me their use will only increase. It is the only way a software company can provide support and stay in business.

I think what we now consider technical support will become more advanced and turn into consulting services provided over the phone line. The phone companies already have done a fabulous job of providing gateways for this service. Many software companies see the key right now as being through the use of paid phone systems like a 900 number.

It is interesting that when a customer is paying for support, he sometimes checks for a README file before calling. On the other end of the line, the support technician is happy to provide whatever hand-holding may be necessary.

Hopefully, the software industry will mature and find a solution to providing support in a fashion the customer appreciates and the software company can run and still be profitable.

Treating the Customer Right

Technical support comes down to one thing: **treating the customer right**. Treat customers how you would like to be treated. Most of the time, the customers will not treat you right, but, of course, they are the customers.

Instead of saying you can't teach them how to program in C, tell them that although you are not set up to teach C programming, the best book you have read about C programming is "Using Borland C++" (from Que). If you can't help them directly, try to provide additional information they can use to find further help.

Conclusion

This chapter examined ways to run a technical support department. It gave ideas to help you make technical support better.

In particular, the following topics were covered:

- The sole purpose of technical support is to provide service, advice, and assistance in the use of a software product to a customer. This assistance can be on any level, all the way from helping a customer install an application which won't install correctly, to providing theoretical assistance on the use of the product.

- The most important aspect of technical support is meeting customer expectations. Meeting customers' expectations means telling the customers what you are going to do for them and then turning around and actually doing what you said you were going to do.

- Anybody working in technical support must understand they are the company's representative. To many customers, the technical support representative *is* the company. Therefore, it is imperative for the technician to act properly, respond appropriately, and interact with the customer in a professional manner.

- You should at least give the impression you are listening to the customers by letting them finish what they are saying before you start speaking. You can also respond by changing the tone of your voice and by acknowledging what the customer is saying.

- The most important element of troubleshooting is asking questions. By asking intelligent questions, you can find the answer to most any problem.

- There are definite ways to make providing technical support easier. It starts by telling the customers what they should already know before calling. When you list a technical support telephone number, ensure that you tell the customer to have pertinent information ready at the time of the call.

- One of the best ways to help the customer is to keep a piece of paper next to your phone. When you are answering questions, and you come across one to which you are not 100 percent sure of the answer, write it down. Then, in your time off the phones, you can research the problem.

- Technical support can be much more then just talking to somebody on the phone. Great technical support staffs provide alternate methods for customers to help themselves. Often, taking telephone calls is the most common aspect of technical support.

- Other ways to help the customer include letters through U.S. mail, or an overnight package carrier (FedEx, Airborne Express, and so on), FAX, and electronic methods such as CompuServe, BIX, Genie, and the Internet.

- A FaxBack service can be an incredibly useful way to provide technical support. You have a toll-free phone number to provide technical documents faxed to the customer at no charge. Customers call and enter the technical information document number with the touch tone pads on their fax machine. The information is then faxed back to the customer immediately.

- Because of the costs involved with technical support, the company you are working for will probably want to minimize the time you spend on each call. A good way to do this is to keep a sheet of paper on your desk on which you can write down the length of the call, and what it was about. If you notice a certain type of call taking a long time, find a way to describe the problem quickly.

- The future of technical support is wrapped in the use of technology to make it easier for the customer to find the solutions to the questions they have. This technology is most likely through the use of electronic services such as CompuServe and electronic BBS systems.

Chapter 10

Wrapping It Up

This chapter covers some miscellaneous topics about software development that didn't fit well in other locations in the book. You learn about working with teams of people and about having successful meetings. We give you tips for managing a team and ideas on getting your software created.

In particular, the following topics are covered in this chapter:

- Tips for holding successful team meetings.
- Ideas for managing a team of programmers.
- Tips on just doing it.

Successful Meetings

Meetings are an important aspect of any business. The purpose of a meeting is to communicate information between members of a team. The result is people having a better awareness of what is happening with a project. Team members should know the reasons why they are attending a meeting.

If you have ever been involved in a meeting, the above paragraph might sound like a fairy tale. Therefore, let's look at some hints at running successful meetings:

- *Have a good agenda.* The agenda should serve as a plan of what you want to discuss in the meeting and what you want to accomplish. You should create an agenda for the meeting before the meeting even starts.

- *Start on time.* Don't wait for people who are late. This only punishes the people who are on time and promotes others to arrive late in the future, knowing in good faith the meeting will be stalled until they arrive.

- *Stay on track.* Follow the agenda you created before the meeting. Team members become tired of a meeting when it gets off the topic originally planned. Now, this isn't to say that you should not discuss other important topics that come up, but remember to respect the team members' schedules by trying to follow the topics you originally planned on.

You should have somebody moderate the meeting. In most companies this usually is either the person who called the meeting or the manager of the group having the meeting (this often is the same person).

Length of Meetings

You will find, as the development of your application progresses from the planning stages to the testing phases, your meetings will evolve along with the application.

During the design stages, meetings are longer and more open-ended. These meetings are intended to generate ideas for the application's internal design. Team members are often thinking of different ways to implement certain features.

At the end of the development process, when most of the application has been written and you are working out the program's bugs, meetings tend to be shorter and more frequent. These meetings focus on bugs that are being ironed out, and since team members are so busy programming, the meetings won't take up any more of their valuable time than necessary.

Alternatives to Meetings

It is not always easy for teams to get together physically. This is the case for teams spread out between buildings or with different work schedules. There are alternatives to meetings that many organizations are finding useful.

> **Note**
>
> At Borland, while we were waiting for our new headquarters to be built, the company was spread out among 21 buildings throughout Scotts Valley, California.

The obvious alternative is using electronic mail. E-mail enables team members to leave and respond to messages at any time of the day. E-mail enables people to be almost anywhere they have access to a phone. With a dial-up e-mail system, you can access your mail from anywhere you can connect another computer to the phone. This can be especially useful for programmers, because everybody knows programmers become more creative as the night gets older.

You can use a type of software generally referred to as *groupware* to help create better meetings. Groupware applications enable users to create forms and databases that many people working on a network can access.

Lotus Notes is probably the most well-known groupware program. Notes is powerful because it provides a way to create mail, forms, and database access that enable users working in a group to share information. That is exactly what the purpose of meetings is, and many companies are finding groupware applications like Notes to be a good alternative to meetings.

> **Note**
>
> At Sony, where we currently work, we use Lotus Notes as a means of tracking bug reports. Anybody can fill out a bug form within Lotus Notes. Then, the developers can access the bug report, make modifications to code, and specify how the bug was resolved.

Another type of groupware product is the scheduling program. Windows for Workgroups (there is that word again) includes an application known as Schedule+ that provides a means for scheduling meetings and keeping track of people's time.

Managing the Team

It is difficult to be a manager. Not only are you responsible for getting tasks done, but you also must put up with the barrage of jokes about managers. If you want to be a good manager, there are entire books on the topic. The bookstores are deluged with business books on being a better manager.

Therefore, this section provides just a couple of tips for managing a team of programmers in a high-technology organization. The first thought would be that managers should be lots of fun. At the same time, a manager should be able to delegate tasks.

Managers also should have the respect of their team members. In a team of programmers, the best way to gain respect is to program code yourself. I don't think there is anything that turns a programmer on more (at least as far as topics we cover in this book) than writing a new algorithm or writing code that implements some new feature. The best way to get the respect of your peers is to be good at what you do.

Note
I once read that people become managers by being good programmers. The ironic fact is they spend a certain length of time at becoming good at programming. They are then rewarded by being given totally new responsibilities as a manager. Often, these responsibilities don't have much to do with programming at all. They have more to do with keeping track of people, writing budgets, and reporting the status of projects to other people in the company. As a result, managers don't get to program, something that they have worked on and studied for a certain length of time. The worst part of the matter is that they can't pass on what they have learned about programming to the junior programmers on their team.

Doing It

Remember the theme "Just Do It" from the Nike Shoes advertisement.

With regards to Nike, software development might be similar to running a race (some might say a marathon). But, for any application of significant size, software development is definitely more complex than a race, because it should be considered a team sport.

Before you actually write the application, you do everything you can to plan it. You must decide how the application looks, how it runs, and what functionality it provides to the user. These are often done with other people's help.

Internally you must decide on the algorithms the application uses, what language you want to use, and even which vendor's compiler you use to do development.

Once you start coding, you must rework algorithms. You must test functions you have written, and you need to coordinate your programming activities with other team members. You also need to work with other departments to coordinate activities. You need to work with marketing to make sure your program will be effectively advertised. Also, you need to work with the documentation department to make sure features of your application are properly documented.

When you have a preliminary copy of your software that has basic functionality intact, you need to work with quality assurance to test the software's features and get feedback from beta testers on what they thought about the application.

After you've finally shipped the product, don't fill your champagne glass too quickly. You must plan for the next version of your product. Most companies know at the time that a product ships what major features will be in the next release of the software.

Do you know what they will be for your application? If you have an application you're sure will grow, you should already be familiar with them. These features are often those that didn't make it into the current release of the software.

At this point, go ahead and sip from that champagne glass. Take it easy for a while. After all, once you start working on the next version, things will be just as busy.

Conclusion

So there you have it. I hope this book has been helpful to you, not only for providing some insight into how software is developed, but also to give you some of our own personal experiences in the software industry.

This chapter covered information that did not fit into other areas of the book. It looked at ways to hold successful meetings, ways to manage a team, and provided an overview to the topics covered in this book.

The following topics were covered in this chapter:

- The purpose of a meeting is to communicate information among team members. Meetings are an important aspect of any business.

- Some hints at running successful meetings include: having a good agenda, starting on time, and staying on track.

- Your meetings evolve along with the application. During the design stages, meetings are longer and more open-ended. At the end of the development process, when most of the application has been written and you are working out the bugs in the program, meetings tend to be shorter and more frequent.

- Some alternatives to meetings include the use of e-mail and groupware programs such as Lotus Notes and Schedule+ from Microsoft.

- It is difficult to be a manager. Some hints on being a good manager include: be lots of fun, be able to delegate tasks, and have the respect of your team members.

- Writing software can be similar to running a race. Sometimes you have to just do it.

Appendix

A Sample Functional Specification

On the following pages of this appendix we want to provide you with an example functional specification. It's taken from a program that may someday be available through shareware. You can use this sample as a template for your own functional specification that you may need to create at some time in the future.

The main things you need to remember to provide in your functional spec are:

- *Screen shots:* Keep in mind that a picture is worth a thousand words, and the more shots you have of what you are talking about in the text, the more you will aid the reader in understanding the functionality of your program.

- *Discuss all interface elements:* It's also important to remember to include all of the interface elements in your discussion. You'll need to explain what the element is used for, how the user interacts with it, what the acceptable input is (if it's known), and what happens when the user interacts with it.

- *Clearly indicate anything that is not yet known:* Sometimes there are things that are not yet finalized when the functional spec is initially written. You should indicate—through special formatting, like italics—everything which is unknown.

The main layout of a functional spec is this:

- Title page

- Table of Contents

- Introductory overview of the main functioning of the program

- For each section:

    - Full-view picture with each interface element labeled

    - Overview of each interface element

    - Discussion of each interface element

In the case of our example functional spec, we have only one screen, so we'll simply present a labeled picture of our screen and discuss each of the interface elements. Since most programs aren't as small and straightforward as this program, usually there will be more sections to the functional specification. With Norton Desktop for Windows, for example, we had a separate section for each of the programs in the entire product. The MediaSurf Functional Spec follows.

MediaSurf—Functional Specification

August 8th, 1994

Revision 1.0

Table of Contents

Introduction

Media Type Dropdown Control Box

Directory/Drive Listbox

File Listbox

Full Path Static Text

File Information Static Text

Media Playback Box

Playback Control Buttons

Play/Pause Button

Stop Button

Position Slider

Hex Display Button

Help Button

Close Button

Introduction

MediaSurf is a program that provides the user with a means of quickly browsing and "viewing" the contents of their multimedia files, such as bitmap, waveform, MIDI, and video files. The "viewing" of the files is actually a playing of the files, and will vary depending on the type of file being played. This functional specification discusses in further detail later what occurs when each of the multimedia file types is played. Information about the file—which, again, varies depending upon the type of file being played—is also presented to the user.

This is the main interface screen of this program and is displayed in Figure A.1. Through it the user can navigate their disks and play the various types of multimedia files they encounter.

Fig. A.1
The Main Screen
of the MediaSurf
Program.

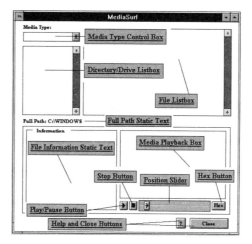

The main interface elements on this screen are:

- Media Type Dropdown Control Box

- Directory/Drive Listbox

- File Listbox

- Full Path Static Text

- File Information Static Text

- File Playback Box

- Playback Control Buttons

- Play/Pause Button

- Stop Button

- Eject Button

- Position Slider

- Hex Display Button

- Help Button

- Close Button

Media Type Dropdown Control Box

The Media Type Dropdown Control Box controls the types of files that display in the File Listbox (see fig. A.2). There are currently five types of multimedia files—listed alphabetically—that can be accessed by MediaSurf:

Fig. A.2
Media Type
Dropdown
Control Box.

- Bitmap (.BMP)

- MIDI (.MID)

- QuickTime for Windows (.MOV)

- Video for Windows (.AVI)

- Waveform (.WAV)

As a standard Windows control box, the Media Type Control Box conforms to the Windows interface guidelines for its usage. The user can drop the control box down by pressing the activator button—the down-arrow button on the right side of the control—with the left mouse button. It also can be activated through the keyboard by pressing the down-arrow key when the media type control box has keyboard input focus. In standard Windows fashion, input focus is indicated by highlighted text in the control box's text edit field.

When the activator button is invoked, the control box drops its list down; within the list is an alphabetical listing of the media types the program supports. The user can select a file type by single-clicking an item with the left mouse button. Through the keyboard, the item is selected by using the up and down keys, then pressing the Enter key to complete the selection.

The following occurs as each of the media types is selected in the media type control box:

Bitmap: The File Listbox is filled with all the files matching the .BMP extension in the current directory of the current drive.

MIDI: The File Listbox is filled with all the files matching the .MID extension in the current directory of the current drive.

QuickTime for Windows: The File Listbox is filled with all the files matching the .MOV extension in the current directory of the current drive.

Video for Windows: The File Listbox is filled with all the files matching the .AVI and other related extensions—like .AVS—in the current directory of the current drive.

Waveform: The File Listbox is filled with all the files matching the .WAV extension in the current directory of the current drive.

Directory/Drive Listbox

The Directory/Drive Listbox enables the user to select a disk drive and directory on a drive on which they can navigate (see fig. A.3). The listbox is filled with all the subdirectories accessible on the current path, followed by an alphabetical listing of all the drives available on the user's system.

The user selects an entry on the list by single-clicking the left mouse button or by pressing the up and down arrows, the page up and page down keys, or the the home and end keys on the keyboard.

Fig. A.3
Directory/Drive
Listbox.

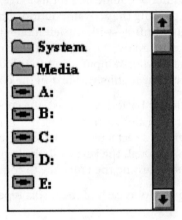

The list also can be navigated with the mouse through the scroll bar. Clicking the up arrow moves the list up one item; clicking the down arrow moves it down one item. Clicking the thumb moves through the list accordingly. Clicking above the thumb moves the list up by one page; clicking below the thumb moves the list down one page.

The user can navigate to a new directory or drive by double-clicking an entry with the left mouse button, or by pressing the Enter key; this invokes the currently highlighted entry.

If the current path is not at the root of the current drive, two dots (..) are used to indicate the parent directory. When the user invokes this entry—either with the mouse or the keyboard—the listbox is filled with the subdirectories of the parent of the current directory.

As the selection in the listbox changes, the File Listbox is updated with the files in the current directory on the current drive; the Full Path Static Text control is updated with the full path—C:\WINDOWS, for example.

File Listbox

The user can select a file for playing from the File Listbox (see fig. A.4). A file is selected by single-clicking the left mouse button, or using the keyboard's up, down, page up, page down, home, and end keys. Further control of the listbox is accomplished with the mouse by left-clicking the scroll bar (see discussion pertaining to using the scroll bar in the Directory/Drive Listbox section for more details).

When a file is selected it is "played." Playing the file includes the following:

- Information about the file is displayed in the File Information Static Text Box

- The file is played. For each of the media types this is what occurs:

   Bitmap Files: The bitmap file is displayed in the Media Playback Box. It is a reduced version of the picture that is fully displayed within the Box's rectangle. All the Playback Control Buttons are disabled.

   The Hex Display button is enabled.

   Video Files (QuickTime and Video for Windows): The video file is displayed in the Media Playback Box. As with bitmap files, it is a reduced version of the movie.

   All the Playback Control Buttons as well as the Hex Display Button are enabled.

   Waveform and MIDI Files: A hexadecimal output of these files' contents is displayed in the Media Playback Box.

   All the Playback Control Buttons are enabled; the Hex Display Button is disabled since there is no option to switch back to a Picture view.

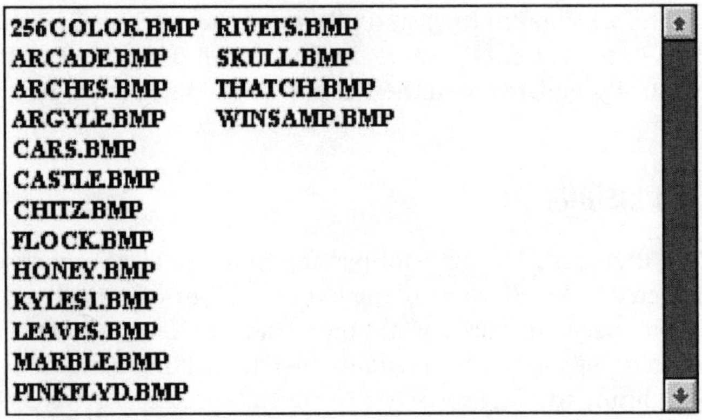

Fig. A.4
File Listbox.

```
256COLOR.BMP   RIVETS.BMP
ARCADE.BMP     SKULL.BMP
ARCHES.BMP     THATCH.BMP
ARGYLE.BMP     WINSAMP.BMP
CARS.BMP
CASTLE.BMP
CHITZ.BMP
FLOCK.BMP
HONEY.BMP
KYLES1.BMP
LEAVES.BMP
MARBLE.BMP
PINKFLYD.BMP
```

Full Path Static Text

The Full Path Static Text control shows the user the current drive and directory path (see fig. A.5). If a file is currently selected in the File Listbox, it is appended to the full path. The format of the display is

```
Drive:\DirectoryPath\FileName
```

There is no user interaction in this control.

Fig. A.5
Full Path Static Text.

Full Path: C:\WINDOWS\WINSAMP.BMP

File Information Static Text

The File Information Static Text box provides the user with pertinent information about the file currently being played (see fig. A.6).

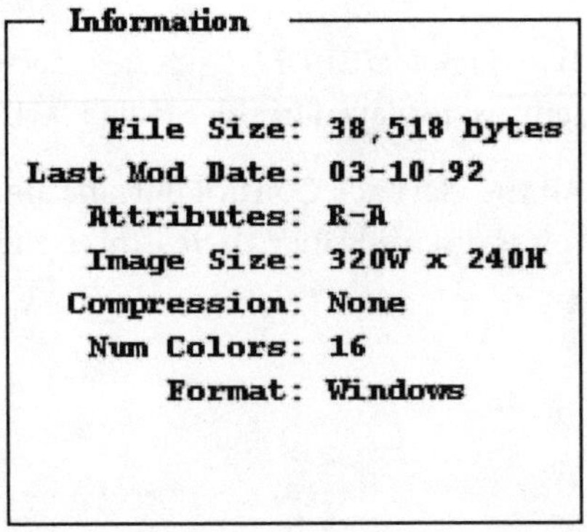

Fig. A.6
File Information
Static Text Box.

```
┌ Information ─────────────────┐
│                              │
│       File Size: 38,518 bytes│
│   Last Mod Date: 03-10-92    │
│      Attributes: R-A         │
│      Image Size: 320W x 240H │
│     Compression: None        │
│      Num Colors: 16          │
│          Format: Windows     │
│                              │
└──────────────────────────────┘
```

A basic set of information about the file is displayed at the top of the box. This is information about the file that is independent of the file's media type. The basic information consists of the following:

Size of File

Last Modification Date

Attributes (read-only, hidden, archived)

The type and amount of other information displayed here varies for each of the media types. The following is a sampling of information which may be displayed for each of the media types. *[Note that details of what is to be displayed have not been finalized for each of the types at the time of this writing. This will be updated as more details are finalized.]*

Bitmap:	
Size	640W x 480H pixels
Compression	None
Num Colors	256 (8-bit)
Format	Windows

MIDI:	
[Yet to be finalized]	

QuickTime for Windows: Video for Windows:	
Duration	46.23 seconds
Size	320W x 240H pixels
Resolution	72 dpi
Num Colors	Millions (24-bit)
Compressor	Cinepak
Channels	Mono
Sampling	8 bits @ 22 kHz

Waveform:	
Channels	Mono
Sampling	8 bits @ 22 kHz

There is no user interaction in this control.

Media Playback Box

The Media Playback Box displays the contents of the file currently being played. For each of the media types this is what occurs:

- *Bitmap Files:* The bitmap file is displayed in the Media Playback Box. It is a reduced version of the picture that is fully displayed within the Box's rectangle. See Figure A.7 for an example of a bitmap displayed in the Playback Box.

Fig. A.7
Media Playback
Box Showing
Bitmap File.

- *Video Files (QuickTime and Video for Windows):* The video file is displayed in the Media Playback Box. As with bitmap files, it is a reduced version of the movie. See Figure A.8 for an example of a video file displayed in the Playback Box.

Fig. A.8
Media Playback Box
Showing Video File.

- *Waveform and MIDI Files:* A hexadecimal output of the contents of these files is displayed in the Media Playback Box. See Figure A.9 for an example of a hexadecimal display of a waveform file in the Playback Box.

There is no user interaction in this control.

Fig. A.9
Media Playback
Box Showing MIDI
File Hexadecimal
Display.

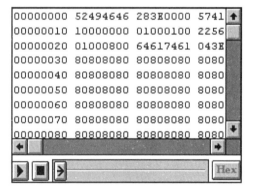

Playback Control Buttons

The Playback Control Buttons allow the user to play, pause, stop, or move to a certain part of the media file currently being played. Playback of all media file types except Bitmap files can be controlled with these buttons:

- *Play/Pause Button:* The Play/Pause Button is a toggle between the Play and Pause states. When the button is in the Play state it is displayed with a sideways triangle and is single-clicked with the left mouse button or when the spacebar is pressed when this button has the input focus, the file is "played" and the state changes to the Pause state; the display of the button changes to the Pause Button that is composed of two vertical bars. Figure A.10 shows the two states of the buttons.

Fig. A.10
Play/Pause Button.

- *Stop Button:* The Stop Button stops the currently playing file. If the file is not currently playing, this button is disabled. Thus, after invoking the button with either a single-click of the left mouse button or pressing the spacebar key when this button has the input focus, the currently playing file stops playing and this button is disabled. Figure A.11 shows the Stop Button in both the enabled—the upper slider—and disabled—the lower slider—states.

Fig. A.11
Stop Button.

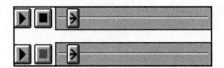

- *Position Slider:* The Position Slider enables the user to set the current play position to anywhere in the file. Interaction with this control is only available through single-clicking the mouse button, in a fashion similar to a scroll bar. The slider is moved by single-clicking, then holding, the Slider Button. Moving the slider to the right moves toward the end of the file; moving the slider to the left moves toward the beginning of the file. Clicking to either the right or the left of the Slider Button jumps to the relative position in the file, toward the end or beginning of the file respectively. Play is automatically continued after the slider has been moved. Figure A.12 details this control.

Fig. A.12
Position Slider.

Hex Display Button

The Hex Display Button enables the user to view a hexadecimal display of the contents of the currently playing file. It is a button that toggles between two states: Hex and Picture view. See Figure A.13 for an example of this button in both states.

Fig. A.13
Hexadecimal
Display Button.

In either state, this button is activated by single-clicking the left mouse button or pressing the spacebar key when the control has the keyboard input focus.

When the button is in Hex state the text on the button is "Hex." Invoking the button when it is in this state causes the display in the Media Playback Box to change to a hexadecimal listing of the contents of the currently selected file from the File Listbox. If the file is currently playing, it is stopped. The button changes to Picture state.

When the button is in Picture state the text on the button is "Pict." Invoking the button when it is in this state causes the display in the Media Playback Box to change to the pictorial display of the currently selected file from the File Listbox. The file is automatically played from the beginning upon activation of this button. The state is changed to Hex state.

Help Button

The Help Button enables the user to access MediaSurf's on-line help. The button is activated by single-clicking the left mouse button or pressing the spacebar key when the control has the keyboard input focus.

When the button is invoked, the standard Windows Help System is launched with MediaSurf's help file displayed.

Close Button

The Close Button terminates the program. It can be invoked either by single-clicking the left mouse button or pressing the spacebar key when the control has the keyboard input. As is standard Windows practice, the program also can be terminated by simultaneously pressing the Alt and F4 keys.

Tab Ordering of the Interface Elements

The tab-key ordering of the elements on the main MediaSurf screen is as follows (see fig. A.14):

Fig. A.14
Tab Ordering
of Elements of
MediaSurf Interface.

1. Media Type Dropdown Control Box

2. Directory/Drive Listbox

3. File Listbox

4. Play/Pause Button

5. Stop Button

6. Hex Display Button

7. Help Button

8. Close Button

Tab-key ordering enables the user to move the keyboard input focus to interface elements within the screen. Movement to the next interface element is
accomplished by pressing the Tab key; movement to the previous interface
element is accomplished by pressing the Shift and Tab keys simultaneously.

When the user is on the last item (the Close Button) and presses the Tab key,
input focus moves to the first interface element (the Media Type Dropdown
Control Box). When the user is on the first item and presses the Shift and Tab
keys simultaneously, input focus moves to the last interface element.

If any of the interface elements is disabled, input focus moves to the next
element that is enabled.

Index